Getting the Buggers to Behave

Third Edition

Other titles by Sue Cowley:

Getting the Buggers to Think – Sue Cowley
Getting the Buggers to Write 2 – Sue Cowley
Guerilla Guide to Teaching – Sue Cowley
How to Survive your First Year in Teaching – Sue Cowley
Letting the Buggers Be Creative – Sue Cowley
Sue Cowley's Teaching Clinic – Sue Cowley
Sue Cowley's A–Z of Teaching – Sue Cowley
Getting Your Little Darlings to Behave – Sue Cowley

Also available in the series:

Getting the Buggers into Languages 2nd Edition – Amanda Barton
Getting the Buggers Fit – Lorraine Cale
Getting the Buggers into Science – Christine Farmery
Getting the Buggers to Turn Up – Ian McCormack
Getting the Buggers to Add Up 3rd Edition – Mike Ollerton
Getting the Buggers to Read – Claire Senior
Getting the Buggers to Do their Homework – Julian Stern

Getting the Buggers to Behave

SUE COWLEY

continuum

Continuum International Publishing Group
The Tower Building   80 Maiden Lane
11 York Road   Suite 704
London SE1 7NX   New York
     NY 10038

www.continuumbooks.com

British Library Cataloguing-in-Publication Data
A catalogue record for this book is available from the British Library.

ISBN: 0–8264–8912–5 (paperback)

Library of Congress Cataloging-in-Publication Data
A catalog record for this book is available from the Library of Congress.

Typeset by BookEns Ltd, Royston, Herts.
Printed and bound in Great Britain by MPG Books Ltd, Bodmin, Cornwall

Contents

Part Two: The Teacher and the Teaching

Part Three: The Students

Part Four: The Wider Environment

Part Five: For Example ...

Part Six: When Things get Tough ...

Acknowledgements

Thanks to all the students who helped with the interviews, especially: Mark, Kirsty, Andrew, Mark, Jason, Paula, Roshney, Sarah, Becky, Nicola, Lisa, Jon, Shaun, Nick, Daniel, Craig, Michael, Nina, Grace, Louise and Lisa. Thanks also to all the teachers who have inspired and helped me in my teaching career – you know who you are!

Thanks to Alexandra Webster and all the team at Continuum. Thanks to all the girls at the October Club for their advice and support. And of course, special thanks to Tilak and Álvie, who make it all possible.

Author's note, third edition

I meet lots of teachers and other school staff through my work, and over the years I've been given loads of great ideas for managing behaviour. I include many of these ideas in this new edition, so a big 'thank you' to anyone whose suggestions I've nicked. Please remember, especially if you're just starting out in teaching, that there is no magic wand when it comes to managing behaviour. (And anyway if there were, life as a teacher would lack the vital 'spark' that makes the job fun and challenging.) What we do have available to us, though, are a huge variety of different strategies, techniques and approaches. That's what you'll find in this book.

Recently, I've been thinking back a lot to my own schooldays. I had some good times, and some good teachers, but what really sticks in my mind are the negative memories. Emotions such as boredom, nervousness, humiliation and even terror. Anyone who harks back to the 'good old days', when students did as they were told without question, should not forget the atmosphere of fear that often prevailed. And those of us who work with children now should never underestimate the kind of impact we as teachers can have on our students, for good or for bad.

A teacher said to me recently that, generally speaking, students misbehave for two reasons: either they are bored, or they don't understand. Although this is clearly a simplification, it does usefully summarize two areas over which the teacher has direct control. We can certainly spice up our teaching to engage with a class – put the fun back into the classroom and show children how exciting and interesting learning can be. And we can also ensure that we make our teaching understandable by, and accessible to, every child in the class. What we can't do is force our children into changing their behaviour (although we can certainly encourage them to make better decisions over time). What we *can* do is change our own behaviour to make life easier and better for us and for our students. Hopefully this book will show you how to change your own behaviour as a teacher for the better.

I've worked in a number of different schools, and it's amazing how what works well in one setting will be totally useless in another. With this in mind, please adapt the advice I give in this book to suit the children with whom you work. Trust your instincts, and keep up the process of learning – be a teacher who never stops developing his or her own practice. And at the toughest moments, never lose sight of the fact that you are doing a really important job, one that can make a genuine difference to people's lives.

Sue Cowley
www.suecowley.co.uk

Behaviour management: if you get it right, your life is easy, you're free to do what you're meant to do, which is of course to teach. With a well-behaved class, teaching is one of the most wonderful jobs in the world. Every day offers you a new and different experience: the chance to see the children discover fresh concepts, to learn something that they never knew before, the opportunity to make a real difference to the lives of your students. As they say, 'nobody forgets a good teacher', but what exactly does being a 'good teacher' mean?

One of the most essential characteristics of a good teacher is the ability to manage our students' behaviour, so that we can help them to learn. This is especially so if you work in a school where there are many behaviour problems. We can only spark that crucial desire to learn if we can first get our children to concentrate, to have self-discipline, to behave themselves! Every student in every school deserves the best education that we can possibly offer them, and we must find a way to achieve this. Some schools and some students prove to be a real challenge for any teacher; and even in schools where poor behaviour isn't a huge problem, there are days when you just can't seem to get it right. This book can help by offering you a wealth of practical ideas to try out in your own classroom, to lend you a hand in 'getting the buggers to behave'.

Teachers use a wide variety of different skills in their everyday work. You need to be a specialist at teaching your subject or subjects, and you must also manage the behaviour of a large number of young people. To a certain extent, teachers learn how to do this through actually being in the classroom, and as time goes on you find yourself drawing from a wide bank of ideas and experiences to help you. There do seem to be some teachers who are naturally good at regulating behaviour, who have an innate ability to engage and 'hold' a class. However, it is also possible to learn how to improve and increase your behaviour management skills, and that is exactly what this book will help you do.

This book is practical, easily accessible and easy to read. No academic theory – just lots of tips, advice, and examples to show how the ideas I give really work in practice. Although I address the ideas to teachers, you might also find this book helpful if you work in other educational settings (as a classroom assistant, as a school librarian, as a lunchtime supervisor, and so on).

Teachers today are stressed, there is no doubt about it. This stress is caused by many different factors – poor behaviour, excessive workload, a lack of status in contrast to other professions. What I offer you in this book are some ways of minimizing the stress. That is why this book focuses mainly on strategies for the *teacher*, rather than for the *student*. What I am interested in doing is helping you as a teacher, helping you survive on a day to day basis in a difficult and challenging job, and allowing you to enjoy the amazing career you have chosen.

This book gives you advice on behaviour management that is easy to understand and equally easy to apply. After all, how many of us, snowed under with reports to write and lessons to plan, have time to wade through endless theory? There is plenty of information on the basics of behaviour management, plus lots of tips for controlling your classes and ideas for managing the physical aspects of the classroom environment. The ideas and advice given are based on common-sense observations and strategies that have worked for me. My hope is that you will find this book a useful reference source in your everyday teaching, one that you can turn to for ideas when you need them, or to find alternative strategies for dealing with the management of your own class or classes.

So, I do hope that this book will help you in getting *your* students to behave. And if we can get it at least partly right, not only will we improve the education of our children, we will also be able to thrive and flourish in the job that we love.

Part One

IN THE
BEGINNING ...

1

THE BASICS OF
BEHAVIOUR
MANAGEMENT

What are the basics?

In this first chapter, I'm going to take a look at the basics, the initial ground rules of behaviour management. These are the fundamentals, the techniques that need to become intuitive if your teaching style is going to encourage consistently good behaviour. Much of what follows is common sense – it's about developing good relationships with your students. But it's all too easy to lose sight of these common-sense approaches when faced with thirty rebellious youngsters.

If you're an experienced teacher you will probably already be using these strategies so automatically that they have become a subconscious part of your teaching. If you are facing some problems (perhaps in a new school or with a particularly tricky class), then you might like to look at the ideas given below to check whether something fairly straightforward is going wrong.

If you're a trainee, or new to the profession, then the basics will give you a good foundation from which to start the process of becoming a really great teacher. Hopefully, I can show you how to match that behaviour management theory you learned in college with the reality of being in the classroom. These basics are ideas developed from my own teaching experiences, and as a result of watching other teachers at work. They are:

Be definite 'I know what I want.'
Be aware 'I know what will happen if I do/don't get what I want.'
Be calm and consistent 'I'm always polite and fair to you.'
Give them structure 'I know where we're going.'
Be positive 'You're doing great.'
Be interested 'You're people as well as students.'
Be flexible 'I know when to bend rather than break.'
Be persistent 'I refuse to give up.'

Be definite

'I know what I want.'
Being definite in your teaching means knowing what you expect from your students. Like predators sensing a weakness in their prey, students seem to be instinctively aware of vulnerability and uncertainty in their teachers. Knowing exactly what you want allows you to communicate an air of confidence to your class. From the moment you walk through the door, you should be so certain of what you want from your students, that there is no room for them to argue, no chance for them to step out of line. And if they do misbehave, this should be treated with a suitable level of amazement and surprise. Your image is of wonderfully behaved children with huge quantities of potential: can it really be that they are not living up to your expectations?

Once you've worked out what you want in your own mind, do make sure that you let your students in on the secret. They can only try to do what you want if you tell them exactly what you do require. Aim to make your decisions before your first lesson with a class, to avoid any suggestion of uncertainty on your part. (This is one of the reasons why behaviour management becomes much easier with experience: you have already made these important decisions in previous years.)

When you first start out in teaching, you might be inclined to play the role of friend rather than authority figure, feeling that it is somehow unfair to make demands of your students. But young people actually *want* certainty from the adult figures in their lives. They need you to create and enforce boundaries that give them a feeling of security. This is perhaps particularly true for your most difficult students, who may lack structure in their home lives, and who may test all the adults that they meet to see what the reaction will be.

Of course, there will be situations and schools where, despite your best efforts, some of the students refuse to comply with your expectations. At these times it can be very tempting to give up, to say 'whatever' and just let the students behave as they wish. But maintaining high standards and *refusing* to give up on your expectations is, in the long run, the key to success as a teacher.

7

So what exactly do you need to be definite about? Your school behaviour policy will give you general guidance on the forms of behaviour that are viewed as unacceptable – chewing gum, using mobile phones, swearing, the classic 'no go' areas. It should also give you a 'code of conduct' or some 'class rules' that you can use to define acceptable behaviour. My personal top three expectations would be:

- *'I expect you to be completely silent when I'm talking, or when anyone is addressing the whole class.'* To my mind, getting this expectation met is absolutely fundamental to our work as teachers.
- *'I expect you to be respectful at all times.'* This is a useful 'catch all' to cover the way that your students treat you, each other, themselves, and their environment.
- *'I expect you to work to the best of your ability.'* This establishes an expectation of hard work, but takes into account children with differing abilities.

In addition to these general behaviours, it also pays to be really specific about every aspect of student behaviour in your lessons. If you don't give exact details of what you want, the children have to work it out for themselves (probably by messing around until you do specify your requirements). Here are some questions that you might want to consider, covering a range of classroom management issues. As you will see, there are a whole range of subtle variations that you might choose, depending on your personal preferences and the type of school in which you work.

1. How should the students enter the room? For example, do they

- line up outside in silence until the teacher arrives;
- gather quietly outside and wait for the teacher to invite them in;
- enter as they arrive if the teacher is in the classroom?

8

2. What do the students do once they are inside your classroom? Do they

- go and stand behind their chairs, and wait for the signal to be seated;
- sit down and wait in silence, with clear desks, for the teacher to take the register;
- sit down, gather equipment, and wait for the lesson to begin;
- in the nursery/primary classroom, collect a reading book, then go to sit on the carpet with legs crossed and arms folded;
- collect any equipment they need and start work immediately?

3. How will the lesson start? Will it be

- with the register being taken;
- with homework being collected in;
- with a starter activity that is already on the desks or the board;
- with a recap of work done previously;
- with the teacher explaining the aims of the lesson?

4. How will the children approach their work? Will it be

- in complete silence at all times;
- chatting quietly with the person sitting next to them;
- talking if the work involves a discussion activity;
- talking as they wish with no restrictions;
- in silence for a period of time, then taking a short break to chat?

5. How will the lesson finish?

- with the students being dismissed a few at a time;
- with the students standing behind their chairs, waiting to be dismissed;
- with the class leaving as soon as the bell goes?

Be aware

'I know what will happen if I do/don't get what I want.'
Hopefully, most (or at least some) of the time, your students will
be meeting your expectations. When this does happen, don't just
breathe a silent sigh of relief and keep quiet in the hope that it
will continue. Acknowledge their good behaviour – reward it to
ensure that it happens again. One of the most valuable rewards
of all, where the class respects the teacher, is the application of
liberal amounts of specific, detailed praise. ('That's brilliant, Year
6, every single one of you is listening really well today. I'm really
pleased with you all.')

Of course, you must also know what you are going to do when
things go wrong, as inevitably they will on occasions. When
teachers face low-level misbehaviour, the instinctive reaction is
often to turn straight to sanctions. Train yourself instead to look
around first for what's going right, highlighting any examples of
correct behaviour. ('That's great, Parminder, you're waiting
silently for the lesson to begin. You obviously want to go to break
on time.')

Clearly, though, there will be occasions when sanctions are
necessary – when the misbehaviour justifies instant punishment.
In these circumstances, you must be fully aware of the options
available to you. Both you and your students must be certain
about this: behaviour 'X' will lead to sanction 'Y' every time it
happens. As with your expectations, it is crucial to let the
students in on the secret by explaining the exact connection
between their misbehaviour and the sanction they will receive if
the behaviour continues. This puts the choice in the hands of the
students: if they understand the rules and the sanctions, it is up
to them whether or not to comply.

If a student does challenge your expectations, try taking the
following steps:

- Be *definite* about what you want, and stick to your demands.
- Remain calm and polite throughout the encounter.
- State your expectations clearly.
- Clarify any possible misunderstandings.

- State how the student's behaviour is not meeting your expectations.
- State what will happen if the student continues to defy you.
- Refuse to be distracted from your original point (for instance by a child who tries to deflect blame on to a classmate).
- Depersonalize the sanction, by making it clear that the student is forcing you to give a punishment, rather than it being personal.
- Aim to sound rather sad or disappointed about actually having to impose the sanction (your expectation was that the student was able to behave much better than this).
- If necessary, apply the sanction.
- If possible, allow the student to 'win' back from their position by offering a 'way out'.

Here's an example to show what I mean.

John arrives at the Drama Studio and walks straight in, without taking off his shoes. The teacher has already set the rule that the students must take off their shoes before entering the room.

Teacher: John, please go back outside and take off your shoes.
John: I can't, Miss.
Teacher: We have a rule in drama that we must take off our shoes.
John: But I've sprained my ankle, Miss. I really can't take them off.
Teacher: Do you have a note about your ankle?
John: No.
Teacher: Then please go back outside and take off your shoes.
John: No. I won't.
Teacher: John, I'm afraid that if you won't take off your shoes, you will force me to give you a detention.
John: That's not fair.
Teacher: John, please go back outside and take off your shoes. Then I won't have to give you a detention.
John: No, I won't take off my shoes.
Teacher: Then I'm afraid you're forcing me to give you a detention for five minutes after the lesson.

11

John: Oh please don't, Miss.
Teacher: Tell you what, John, go and take your shoes off right now and behave really well during the lesson, and I'll probably be able to forget that detention. OK?
John: All right then.

Just to show how differently this encounter might have turned out if the teacher didn't follow the guidelines, let's rerun the scene . . .

Teacher: John, go back outside and take off your shoes.
John: I can't, Miss.
Teacher: What do you mean, 'I can't'? Of course you can.
John: But I've sprained my ankle, Miss. I really can't take them off.
Teacher: Don't be so stupid.
John: Don't call me stupid.
Teacher: Look, just go outside and take off your shoes. Now!
John: No. I won't.
Teacher: Then you've got a detention with me after school.
John: That's not fair. I'm not coming. Get stuffed!

Be calm and consistent

'I'm always polite and fair to you.'
All of us welcome calmness and consistency: we like to know what to expect from the people in our lives, and it throws us if we get an unpredictable response. For some poorly behaved children, this is the problem they face at home – they never know what the reaction to their behaviour (good or bad) will be. Our duty as professionals is to provide our students with a calm, consistent and considered role model of adult behaviour and responses.

It's not easy for teachers to be fair and polite all the time – staying calm in the face of misbehaviour can be very hard. This is because of the fight or flight response. The student or class 'attacks' the teacher by messing around. The teacher experiences a rush of adrenaline and feels the urge to attack back. Alternatively, the teacher wants to run away from the situation. Neither of these options is available to us – we can't lash out, and we can't leave.

Although it's difficult, the hard truth is that, if you can remain tirelessly calm and consistent at all times, there will be far less possibility of serious confrontation. You will also avoid creating unnecessary stress for yourself An excellent rule of thumb is to treat your children as you would treat another adult, for instance if you worked in an office, no matter how poorly they behave towards you.

Children are extremely sensitive to the idea of fairness. Students will often complain that they are unfairly singled out and that, once they have misbehaved, they get picked on over and over again. If we are honest, it's only natural that we like some students more than others. The secret, of course, is to treat all children equally despite any personal preferences.

In the secondary school, consistency is a kind of 'holy grail' for headteachers and senior managers, and with good reason. Where the staff apply school rules, rewards and sanctions in a completely consistent way, the students are presented with a single set of standards. But if behaviour 'X' is okay with one teacher and not with another, then the students get confused about where the boundaries actually lie. Of course it is only natural that teachers will sometimes bend and adapt the rules to best suit their own styles or situations. However, do bear in mind that being consistent is actually the fairest approach for your children.

Give them structure

'I know where we're going.'
Our natural impulse is to place a structure on our lives – a daily pattern that gives us a feeling of safety and security. For the most difficult students in our schools, this structure is probably what is missing from their worlds. At home, their parents or guardians may not have set boundaries for them, or they may constantly

move the goalposts, reacting in a variety of different ways to the same types of misbehaviour. Schools offer these young people a refuge, a place where they meet adults who give them suitable and consistent guidelines about what good behaviour actually is.

There are lots of ways that teachers can offer structure to their students: through clear lesson content, through classroom organization, through the methods used to control behaviour. Once you have a clear structure in your own mind, this clarity will be apparent to your class through your high level of awareness and confidence. In addition, make it clear to your students at every stage exactly how and why structures are being used.

If you can achieve a sense of purpose, clarity and structure, this has a number of important benefits:

- Your students know what to expect when they come to your lessons.
- If their expectations are met every time they meet you, they begin to view you as a stable feature of their lives.
- This sense of stability leads to increased trust and better relationships.
- They start to look forward to spending time with you.
- Their behaviour becomes much more predictable and controllable.
- Patterns of good behaviour will be repeated because of the structured environment that you offer.
- Eventually, these behaviours become like habits or reflex actions, requiring little or no input from the teacher.
- The students begin to repeat the patterns automatically, sometimes even without the teacher being present (for instance, lining up outside to wait if you are unavoidably late to the lesson).
- The teacher can start to use quick non-verbal signals to indicate his or her wishes to the class (e.g. a hand signal at the end of the lesson to show that the children should stand behind their chairs).

Here are some areas of your teaching that you can structure, and some examples of possible approaches that you might use:

- *The way that your lessons start:* With the class lined up outside, with the teacher taking the register, with the class doing a starter activity.
- *Where the students sit:* In rows or groups, using a seating plan.
- *What happens during the lesson:* A mix of activities, lots of practical work, starting off with a brainstorm.
- *How resources and equipment are handled:* Students to collect their own books/equipment, specific children to hand out books, equipment kept in one area of the room, resources tidied away by volunteers.
- *Expected working behaviours:* Students working quietly, staying in their seats, putting up hands if they have questions or wish to give an answer.
- *The way that your lessons finish:* With a plenary, with homework being set, students standing behind chairs, sitting in silence for a few moments while the teacher summarizes the lesson, playing a short game.

Be positive

'You're doing great!'
Every teacher knows the mantra, 'stress the positive'. To be honest, it can sometimes feel as though we are praising our students for just about anything, to try to get them 'on our side'. But this is a mistake: if we set our sights low, then this low level is where our students will aim. If we have high standards, and expect great things, our students learn to strive for their best. Being positive is not just about praising your students, it is also about having a positive outlook during your time with them. The discriminating use of praise, and the ability to remain relentlessly positive, will help you a great deal in managing behaviour. It should also make you less susceptible to stress and negative emotions.

Here are a few tips for staying positive with your students:

- always greet your class with a positive expectation, such as 'I just know you're going to do some fantastic work today';

15

- expect the best from your children, rather than anticipating the worst;
- frame everything you say in a positive light;
- try to avoid accusing your students or criticizing them;
- try not to use sarcasm (no matter how tempted you are) – it is 'the lowest form of wit', and can hurt or confuse children;
- react to misbehaviour by suggesting a positive alternative;
- use praise of individuals to encourage the whole class;
- use rewards in preference to sanctions as far as possible;
- constantly set targets to offer positive ways for your students to improve;
- see completion of targets as a chance to give a reward.

Here are two examples of the same situation, a teacher inviting a class into the room, to show the difference between a positive and a negative approach.

Negative

'Come on, hurry up! Why are you being so slow? Come on, come on, we've got loads to get through today and we'll never get everything done if you're this slow. What's wrong with you? Why are you making so much noise?'
I know how I'd feel about being in this teacher's class – inclined to misbehave! Immediately, the students are criticized for being slow. The teacher then creates a negative feeling about the work they will be doing, by putting the blame on the students for not being able to get through it all. Finally, she uses two negative questions to suggest that the students are always this bad. By starting the lesson in such a negative frame of mind, the teacher's expectations may well be met.

Positive

'Right, if you can all come in as quickly as possible. I've got some really exciting things for you to do today, and we need to get started straight away, so that we can get through them all. That's an excellent level of noise. Well done. Now let's see if you can be even quieter.'

16

Here, the teacher tells the students how she wants them to come into the room. She then creates a sense of purpose and interest, by telling them that she has some 'really exciting' things planned for them. Finally, she praises them for the low level of noise, but sets them the challenge of being even quieter. By starting the lesson in this way, a positive atmosphere will hopefully be created and sustained.

Be interested

'You're people as well as students.'
At its heart, good behaviour management is about good teacher/ student relationships. After all, you hopefully came into teaching at least partly because you love working with children or young people. If your students respect you, and feel that you respect them, this will inevitably lead to better behaviour in your classroom. A key part of building respect is to take an interest in what makes your students tick – to care about what makes them remarkable as individual people, as well as them just being students passing through your bit of the education system.

Taking an interest in your students is particularly helpful when you are experiencing behaviour problems. If a whole class is messing you around because they find a topic or subject boring, then you might be able to incorporate some elements of the latest toy or game fad into your lessons. (I suspect that a fair few maths teachers have used the game Sudoku as a way of engaging their students' interest.) If an individual child is giving you grief, then taking an interest in what motivates that student could help you in devising a suitable reward system.

Here are a few suggestions on making better connections with your students:

- *Ask them about their interests:* In the course of your first few meetings with a class, spend some time getting to know more about the students' interests, hobbies, likes and dislikes.
- *Get involved in extra-curricular activities:* If you can spare the time, take part in some activities outside the normal school

day. They give you a great chance to get to know some students better, and to allow the children a glimpse of you the person as well as you the teacher. Although extra-curricular activities are time consuming, my experience has been that participation is more than worth the effort involved.

− *Keep up to date:* You don't actually have to participate in the latest crazes, watch the current hot TV show, read the most recent Harry Potter, or listen to the latest music. But if you can demonstrate at least a passing interest in contemporary culture, this will give you access to a key aspect of your students' lives.

Be flexible

'I know when to bend rather than break.'

There are times as a teacher when you need to learn how to bend a little, for your students' sake and also for your own. Achieving a balance between this flexibility, and the certainty, clarity and consistency already discussed, is one of the hardest and most subtle of all teaching skills. Sometimes, and only sometimes, you will need to relax your boundaries and accept that you are not going to achieve everything that you had initially hoped. By giving a little leeway when it is appropriate, your students will develop greater respect for you as a person and as a teacher.

A flexible approach will mean you tend to find more inventive and interesting ways around any potential problems. Rather than coming at an issue head-on, and refusing to budge or adapt, be willing to take a lateral approach if that is going to work better. It's about being flexible in your thinking, and in your teaching, to help you manage behaviour. For instance, say you have a class who are always tricky last thing on a Thursday afternoon, partly because they are tired, and also because they are timetabled in a small and rundown classroom. You might battle on regardless, handing out loads of sanctions and consequently damaging the relationships you normally have with these students. Alternatively, you might apply a bit of flexibility and take them into the hall or playground for these lessons, doing practical rather than written work.

Flexibility is very much a matter of personal taste and individual circumstances – about knowing when it is appropriate to compromise. In some schools, the children will respond very well to a teacher who bends a little on occasions; at other schools, the students will see any flexibility as a cue to start pushing at the boundaries. In some very challenging situations, where misbehaviour is a complex and deep-rooted issue, taking a 'zero tolerance' approach would mean being left with only a handful of children to actually teach. Here are a few ideas about how and when you could offer your students flexibility:

- *With the class:* If your class is never in the mood for work on Friday afternoons, you will achieve very little if you cannot learn to be flexible. Accept, in your mind, that this situation is outside your control. Aim to achieve a very reasonable amount of work with the class, negotiating targets and talking about how fair you are being. Alternatively, many primary teachers will set this time up as a reward, using a period of 'golden time' last lesson of the week to help them manage behaviour in other lessons.
- *With the work:* On rare occasions, when your class has a good reason not to be in the mood to work, then you might like to offer a compromise. If the students can complete a specified part of the work, you could allow them to chat quietly for a few minutes at the end of the lesson as a reward.
- *With the individual:* Some students simply do not want to be in school: it seems entirely irrelevant to their lives. In these situations, find a balance – set small and achievable targets, but don't beat yourself up if a child does decide to completely opt out. Where a very troubled student is always confrontational with you, particularly when you use sanctions, then try backing off for a while to give you both a break.

Be persistent

'I refuse to give up.'
The ideas and approaches that I give in this book are not a magic panacea – a formula that guarantees instant success. There is no such thing when it comes to managing behaviour, because you are working with the complex nature of human beings. Even if you put all the advice in this book into practice, you will probably still experience some problems with behaviour, at least at first. This is where being persistent comes in – don't give up on the strategies because they don't work immediately. All the time you are working on your behaviour management skills, you will be becoming a better, more effective teacher.

In some very challenging schools, where getting good behaviour is a constant battle, there may be days when you feel like throwing in the towel. It can be very tempting indeed to give up on your key expectations, simply because there is so much disruption going on that you don't know where to begin. But the moment that the students see you think 'talk while I talk, I don't care' or 'it doesn't matter if you're disrespectful', then you are effectively giving up on them.

Sometimes you may come across a 'nightmare class'. A class which, for some reason, seems to contain a large number of really difficult students. In these situations it can prove very hard to keep going, to keep plugging away at behaviour and insisting on certain standards. Do try, though, while at the same time making life a little easier for yourself whenever you can.

Similarly, some children will apparently throw all your efforts straight back in your face. No matter how hard you try to get through to them, it seems like wasted energy. Try not to lose sight of the fact that some children do have pretty horrible lives outside of school. You may be the only adult with whom it is safe to let off steam. Try as hard as you can not to give up on the child who always pushes you away, but do learn to accept that you cannot change the world.

2

Managing the First Meeting

Why is the first meeting so important?

Your first meeting with any class offers you the chance to sow the seeds for an easy year, or to take the first step on the road to disaster. Every teacher must surely know that hollow feeling in the pit of the stomach, as you let a new class into your room, aware that what you do in that first meeting will have such a long-term impact. Often, both the teacher and the students will be feeling at their most defensive in the first lesson together. You may be anticipating poor behaviour from a 'difficult' group of students; they may be expecting you to dislike them if they know that other teachers have found them to be a problem.

With many classes, the first few meetings offer you a 'honeymoon period', where your students are getting to know you, checking you out before revealing their true colours. If this is the type of class you have, try not to start out with an overly relaxed attitude. You may find that, a few lessons into the year, the students start to take advantage of your relaxed approach and begin to misbehave.

On the other hand, you may find yourself in a school where the students will misbehave for new teachers, testing them to see whether they can withstand the ordeal. This is obviously a difficult situation, because it's hard to establish your expectations of behaviour with a class who refuse to listen. If you do find yourself at this type of school, you should very quickly turn to others to help and support you.

What do you need to know before the first meeting?

Teachers are put in a difficult position at the start of a school year (or at the start of the term, if they begin a new job midway through the year). We are expected to meet, control and teach a group of young people about whom we know little or nothing. Because of this, there can be a tendency to learn by our mistakes, dealing with problems as they arise, rather than anticipating and trying to resolve them beforehand.

Time is very precious at the start of term, and staff are busy setting up their classrooms, planning lessons, emptying out pigeonholes, and so on. However, because of the vital importance of this first meeting with your new class or classes, it really is worthwhile taking some time to prepare. Here are some ideas about what you should do in advance of meeting your classes:

- *Possible behaviour problems:* Find out about any well-known troublemakers in the class. If you do know the child's name, and what is likely to set him or her off, you can keep an eye out for the early signs of boundary testing. Sometimes, difficult students will claim to be proud of their reputations. Try turning this situation on its head: 'Jason, great to meet you, I've heard so many good things about you. I'm really looking forward to teaching you.' Give children the chance of a fresh start, by pointing out that you will judge them solely on how they behave and work for you.
- *Learning needs:* Find out whether there are any students in the class who have non-behavioural special needs that may have an impact on their learning. (You should be given a list of those children with special educational needs (SEN), and details of what these needs are. If you are not, approach staff responsible for SEN for this information.) Special needs can be perceived incorrectly by the teacher, and wrongly interpreted as a behavioural issue. For instance, students with literacy problems may not complete the work you set in the time available. If you misinterpret this as laziness, you could provoke misbehaviour.
- *Physical needs:* Find out about any students with physical difficulties and take these children into consideration. Don't assume that your students will be confident enough to tell you about their needs, particularly the youngest ones. Physical needs might include children with hearing difficulties or visual impairment. Adapt seating arrangements for any children who need to be close to the front of the room, and look at your lesson planning to ensure that the work is suitable for everyone.
- *Knowing the names:* It is very useful to know the names of one

or two of your students – the class will be amazed and impressed if you can use a name correctly, apparently without ever having been told it. Even better, if you're good at memory tricks, you might learn the names of the whole class, and claim to be a magician ('Is there a Jasmine in this class? And a Jade? And a Jack?'). Knowing your students' names really is vital for good behaviour management, so make a start on learning them as soon as possible.

While pursuing knowledge is very useful, remember never to prejudge a class. This is likely to put you in a negative frame of mind and it is also unfair on the students. Some children who have a bad reputation in a school are never given a chance to prove this reputation to be false. Tell the class you hope they will impress you and you may be pleasantly surprised.

Establishing your teaching style

The more experienced you become as a teacher, the clearer you will be about the teaching style you are going to use. To an extent, developing your teaching style is something that comes with practice. But before you meet a class for the first time, you should have at least some idea about the style of teaching you will offer them. After all, from the very first moment they meet you, your children will be making decisions about you, based on the signals your teaching style sends.

You will need to adapt the style that you use according to your individual situation. There are many possible variables: the type of school, the age of the children, the teacher's personality, and so on and on. I explore the concept of teaching styles in much more detail in Chapter 5. Here are a few areas of your style that will be under immediate examination in your first lesson:

- *The way you appear:* Are you smart, wearing a suit, or do you dress casually? Do you seem ready to meet and teach the class, or are you flustered and bad tempered when they arrive? Interviewers make their minds up about a candidate in the first few minutes of an interview, based mainly on how they look. If you want your class to behave, you need to make a good impression at this first meeting.

- *The way you talk:* Do you speak with a relaxed, conversational tone? Does your voice sound timid, or conversely too loud? Do you use a good range of tones and different paces to give interest to your speech? Our voices give away huge amounts about our emotional states, especially when we are tense or under stress.
- *The way you stand and move:* Do you look relaxed and make good use of the classroom space? Or do you stand frozen at the front, backed up against the whiteboard in a defensive posture? Does your body language signal aggression or self-confidence? Your children will be reading these signals subconsciously to help them decide how to behave.
- *The way you treat your students:* Do you regard your students as equals, or do you take an authoritarian approach? Do you respect them and talk to them politely, whatever the provocation? Do you remain calm when handling any incidents? Remember, when you are working with and disciplining individual students, your whole class might be watching. They will be making decisions, based on what they see, about how to behave for you in the future.
- *The way you start and finish your lessons:* Are you unprepared and flustered when the children arrive? Do you run out of time at the end of the lesson and let them rush out of the room when the bell goes? Or does your lesson begin and end in a calm and controlled manner? Do you put the children in a good mood from the first minute they meet you? And do they leave you feeling that they have had a positive experience, one that they want to repeat?
- *The way you teach your lessons:* Is the lesson varied, interesting, challenging and fun? Or do you talk at the class for far too long, so that they get bored and start to mess around? I know you can't make every single lesson totally engaging, but try hard to make your first one really great. If you can captivate your students early on, they will come to your class in a constructive frame of mind, ready and eager to learn.

25

- *The way you control the class:* Are you a 'strict and scary' teacher, who shouts at the class from the very first moment you meet them? Are you 'firm but fun', controlling them through the subtle strength of your personality? Or do you greet them timidly, immediately allowing them to feel that they are in charge and not you?

Establishing your expectations

Having clear expectations, and sharing these with the class, is a key part of effective behaviour management. In the first lesson you will be defining the boundaries – 'this is acceptable behaviour and this is not'. Establishing your expectations shows that you are fully in charge of your classroom. Children really do want and appreciate this sense of certainty and clarity.

An excellent way to explain your expectations is to use 'I expect' statements. You might choose three statements from the list below to discuss with your students the first time you meet them. You could then spend some time talking about why these expectations are important. Make sure your statements are as clear and specific as possible, setting positive targets for what you want the children to do, rather than negative statements about what you don't. Here are some suggestions for 'I expect' statements:

- 'I expect you all to line up outside the room in silence before I allow you in.'
- 'I expect you to listen to me (and each other) in complete silence, and paying full attention.'
- 'I expect you to stay in your seats at all times, unless you have permission to get up.'
- 'I expect you always to work to the absolute best of your ability.'
- 'I expect you to show respect for everyone in our class, using appropriate language at all times.'

High expectations are a wonderfully powerful tool in gaining good behaviour and hard work from your children, because they demonstrate your faith in the potential of every single member of your class. There's an excellent example of this in the film *Dangerous Minds*. The teacher (Michelle Pfeiffer) begins her first lesson by telling her class of disaffected students that they all have a grade 'A'. When this statement is greeted with shouts of derision, she explains that they do have an 'A', it's just that it's up to them whether they keep it or lose it.

Here are some useful tips for establishing your expectations:

- *Talk about it!:* Spend plenty of time talking to and with the class about what you want. Ask the students what they feel constitutes acceptable behaviour, but have your own ideas and make sure you get these across. Talk about your most crucial expectations as a key part of your first lesson with a class, then revisit these key points every time you meet.
- *Don't give too many at once:* It's a mistake to give out long lists of demands in your first lesson – the students won't be able to retain them and many will simply switch off. Work out your key expectations (between three and five) and establish these first of all.
- *Use a 'drip feed' approach:* Introduce further expectations as appropriate, over the course of the next few lessons. Link up your expectations with the relevant activity. For instance, the first time you use group work, this gives you the chance to establish the expected behaviour.
- *Match your phrasing to the class:* Adapt the way you explain your expectations depending on the age and attitude of your students. Typically, the younger the children, the firmer you can be – and my advice would be to be as strict as you feel you can get away with! When teaching primary or first year secondary students, use the 'I expect ...' statements (as explained above) and then list the required behaviours. As students get older, you may need to be subtler, *asking* rather than telling them what you want them to do. This is all part of establishing a good working partnership with young adults. I tend to use 'I want' statements with Year 9 students, then 'I need ...' statements with GCSE groups and above.

Establishing the pattern of your lessons

The first lesson is a stressful experience for both teacher and students, because there are so many unknown factors involved. One good way of making the situation feel more controlled is to establish a clear lesson structure or pattern as soon as you can. Probably the best way to illustrate what I mean by 'pattern' is to give an example.

Here is an account of one way of doing things. This lesson lasts one hour and I have given comments about why this particular pattern is used. As you will see, it is first thing in the morning. Mr Charman is at his freshest, ready for this first meeting, and the class is fairly amenable. Please note that this example is not being presented as an ideal lesson, just as one illustration of a possible lesson pattern:

9.00: The bell goes. Mr Charman checks that he has everything ready, then goes to wait outside the room, closing the door behind him.

> **Comment:** The teacher starts the lesson by indicating his status and marking his territory. Standing outside the room, with the door closed, means that he creates a physical and mental barrier between the students and his space. He is well prepared for the actual teaching.

9.03: The students arrive at the classroom in dribs and drabs. Mr Charman is standing waiting for them at the door, arms folded. He is clearly ready for them, and looks imposing. Quietly, he asks the students to line up, in single file, until everyone arrives.

> **Comment:** The pattern for every lesson is being set. The class will line up outside the room until they have all arrived, a useful way of imposing order. As yet, Mr Charman has not addressed the class as a whole. He is waiting to do this until the majority arrive.

9.07: Mr Charman looks very deliberately at his watch. He is now ready to begin. He gets the students silent, then talks to them briefly about what they should do once inside the room.

> **Comment:** The teacher has been quite lenient with the time here, as he does not want to set up confrontations at the start of his first lesson. However, he will explain his exact requirements for the future once the class are inside the room.

9.10: The class are settled in their seats, and Mr Charman begins by explaining how his lessons will run. He sets some boundaries and makes it clear why these are necessary.

> **Comment:** Although the teacher will normally go straight into teaching the content of his lessons, he has a little leeway during this first meeting, when the class are willing to listen to him, to find out what he has to say. He uses this opportunity to make his boundaries very clear, while his students are at their most receptive.

9.15: Now Mr Charman begins the lesson proper. He takes out a £5 note and asks the class what it is. When they tell him that it is worth five pounds, and could he please give it to them, he expresses surprise. *'But it's just a piece of paper, isn't it!'* he says, and starts to tear it into tiny pieces.

> **Comment:** The teacher will certainly have got the class's attention by doing this. (And don't worry, the £5 note is, of course, a fake.) The students will now be engaged and keen to find out what the lesson is going to be about. They will probably also discuss the lesson with other students after it is over, a very useful way of earning yourself a reputation.

9.20: Mr Charman now explains the aim of this particular lesson, which is an exploration of the role of money in society, different currencies, and so on. The class are set a discussion task, which will take them ten minutes.

9.30: The class finish the discussion task and share what they have brainstormed.

9.40: Mr Charman sets a brief written task, which will be completed for homework.

> **Comment:** The pattern of this teacher's lessons is being set. He will start every lesson by explaining the work he aims to do. His classes will include a lot of variety and keep the students' interest throughout. Today, he uses an introduction (teacher addressing class); a period for the students to brainstorm what they already know (group discussion); a session for the class to share what they have discussed (teacher leading with the students listening to each other); and then a written task to reinforce the learning (individual written work), with homework to complete.

9.53: Because this is the first lesson, the teacher leaves plenty of time for clearing up. He stops the class, gets silence, and then explains the pattern for the end of every lesson. The students will write their homework down and then clear away any equipment one table at a time.

9.57: The students have now put the resources away, and the teacher gets silence, then asks them to stand behind their chairs. He then praises them for the excellent work they have done.

> **Comment:** By ending early, Mr Charman has time to praise his students for their hard work, setting up a good feeling about the time they have spent together. He can also make clear his expectations about the completion of homework, or answer any last-minute queries.

10.00: When the bell goes, Mr Charman lets the best-behaved/ hardest-working students go first, praising them as they leave.

> **Comment:** Finally, the teacher shows how to earn the 'reward' of being first to leave – by working hard and behaving well. The lesson finishes in a calm, orderly way, leaving the students with a good impression for next time they meet.

Learning names

Our names are a fundamental part of what makes us who we are, and they offer a very powerful tool in managing behaviour. Knowing and using a person's name helps to gain his or her attention, shows a high level of awareness, and also demonstrates respect. When endeavouring to control student behaviour, you are at a great disadvantage if you do not know the names of the people in your classes. All too often, I have seen (and experienced when doing supply) students taking advantage of a teacher who does not know their names.

If you do not know a student's correct name, it is hard to call him or her back to serve a detention. You are also unable to report the child for poor behaviour. When you do know names, you can give specific praise, point out an individual who is working well, and generally establish much better relationships with a class.

There are various ways of learning your students' names quickly. Here are some ideas that you could incorporate into your first meeting:

- *Use a seating plan:* Not only is using a seating plan a good way of learning names, it is also excellent for demonstrating and keeping control over a class. In the interviews that I conducted with students, this was a feature that came up several times when they were describing 'a teacher who is good at keeping control'. Using a seating plan sends out a definite signal about your style – structured, orderly, in charge. You can also use 'being allowed to sit where you want' as a potential reward for consistent good behaviour.

- *Use memory systems:* Memory systems really are a very useful asset for teachers, particularly when learning names. The basic idea is the use of 'hooks', or connections between things (see Tony Buzan's books for details of various techniques). You might have a student called David who looks a little like a well-known footballer, or you could teach a child named Ben, who is very big (think 'Big Ben').
- *Make notes on your register:* A few subtle annotations on your class lists can help you learn names. When you take the register, look to see whether students have a particular distinguishing characteristic (such as wearing glasses), making a brief note of this to help you remember names. Don't write anything embarrassing or rude, in case someone else takes a look at your planner or mark book!
- *Set yourself a target:* Faced with a sea of children, the task of learning all those names can seem huge, especially if you are a secondary school teacher, perhaps teaching hundreds of different students. Set yourself a reasonable target, aiming to learn three to five names per lesson: within a few weeks you should have learnt the names of all your students.
- *Do some name activities:* Spend some time working on name-specific activities in your first couple of lessons. Ask your children to make decorated name plates to sit on their desks, or to wear sticky name labels. Get the students writing an acrostic poem, using the first letters of their names to start each line. Ask the children to talk about their names to the class: whether they like the name, who chose it, why they were given this name, and so on.

When you are teaching a class with poorly behaved students in it, it is tempting to focus on the troublemakers, learning these children's names first. As a result, you might never get to learn the names of the quiet students. I've certainly made this mistake in the past. Focus on at least one or two quiet students in your first meeting, getting to know these individuals as well.

Reducing the stress of the first meeting

Although the first lesson can be very stressful remember that, as yet, the students will have formed little or no opinion of you. If you are an old hand at your school, your reputation will precede you, particularly if there are the siblings of students you have already taught in the class. If you are a new teacher at the school, you are currently the 'mystery man or woman', an unknown entity, and consequently of great interest. Most older students seem to have an uncanny ability to identify (and subsequently to be difficult for) trainee teachers. Unfortunately, there isn't really an ideal answer to the question: 'Are you a student teacher?'

If the class do misbehave, you might find that your confidence drops and defensiveness takes over, especially in your first lesson. Here are a few tips for reducing the stress if this does happen:

- *Stay calm and relaxed:* If the students see you becoming tense and angry, you are giving them an incentive to misbehave in future. An explosive reaction could be just what they want to get from you. However hard it is (and I know it's hard) you must stay calm. Breathe deeply, pull yourself together, and deal with it.
- *React from the head:* As you feel yourself tensing up, and reacting emotionally rather than intellectually, make a conscious decision not to let your heart win the day. There is a more detailed explanation of this idea in Chapter 18.
- *Don't become defensive:* Remind yourself constantly that this is *not* personal. If your students 'attack' your lesson by misbehaving, do not respond by defending yourself and becoming overly hostile. It's far more useful to attack back by being relentlessly positive.
- *Follow the 'basic rules':* Particularly the first three – be definite, be aware, and be calm and consistent.

And if all else fails . . .

- *Don't be a perfectionist:* Let's face it, it is not a total disaster if a few students muck around in your first lesson. The world is not going to end. You are not going to get the sack. You will learn some valuable lessons from the experience. And you will have plenty of time to win the class back.

3

KEY
STRATEGIES AND
TECHNIQUES

How do I gain and keep control?

It's worth considering why we actually need to control our children's behaviour in the first place. Obviously, it's important for safety reasons, but actually the main reason that we need good behaviour is so that the students can get on with learning. Knowing how to manage behaviour is not about being some kind of control freak, it's done simply so that you can get on with the job of teaching. The more strategies that you have at your disposal to achieve this control, the more confident you will feel. When things are going wrong, you will be able to try one approach after another, until you find something that works for you.

Controlling a large group of people is difficult in any situation, but when some of your students have no wish to be in school, let alone in your lesson, life can become very difficult indeed. In addition to using the basic techniques described in Chapter 1, there are various other ways that you can create and maintain an ordered yet relaxed atmosphere in your classroom. The ten strategies described below are relatively easy to understand and apply, and should hopefully cost you little in the way of stress.

- Learn to 'read' the class
- Wait for silence
- Make use of cues
- Give them 'the choice'
- Be reasonable, *but don't reason with them*
- Use statements, not questions
- Use repetition
- Set targets and time limits
- Use humour
- Put yourself in their shoes

Learn to 'read' the class

As well as being made up of individuals, a class is also an entity in its own right. There will be some days when a class is easy to manage, other days when that exact same class is a nightmare to handle. There are a wide range of factors that can affect the behaviour of a class, and these include:

- The time of the day;
- The day of the week;
- The weather (watch out for those windy or rainy days);
- The presence or absence of certain individuals;
- What happened in the previous lesson;
- Any playground incidents at break or lunchtime;
- The teaching space you are working in;
- The topic area being covered;
- The mood of the teacher;
- Outside events (e.g. an important football match on TV that evening).

The ability to 'read' a class involves using the flexibility discussed in the first chapter. It is a subtle skill to learn, and one that comes more easily with experience. You need to be making on the spot judgements throughout the lesson as to how well your approaches are working. It might be that you have to adapt a lesson activity to better suit the mood of the class; you might have to be a little bit flexible about applying sanctions on a day when there are already high levels of tension in the class.

Knowing how to 'read' a class is especially important for supply teachers, or for secondary staff covering a lesson with a class they do not know. In the first few minutes of a lesson with a cover teacher, the students will be making snap judgements about how they are going to behave. At the same time you need to be making instant decisions about the appropriate style to use with this particular class. Too strict and you will set yourself up for unnecessary confrontations; too liberal and the students are likely to take advantage.

Wait for silence

Waiting for silence is one of the most important control techniques that a teacher can use. When I say 'wait for silence', what I mean is that you should not address your students until they are *completely* silent and fully focused on you. This applies not only at the start of the day or lesson, for instance when taking the register, but also at any time when you wish to talk to the class.

Having silent attention sends a very clear message: the learning is important and you will not allow it to be jeopardized. If the students are talking over you, they will not hear your explanations or instructions. I do understand just how tough it can be to get this silence, but consider the signals you are sending if you do allow students to talk over you. You are basically saying, 'Go ahead and talk, I don't mind.'

In your quest to get silence from a class, it is better if possible to use non-verbal, rather than verbal, techniques. These put less stress on the teacher and add less noise to the classroom. They also give a sense of control, and of teacher confidence. There really is nothing worse than the teacher shouting over the class 'Be quiet! Be quiet!' – it shows that the students are in charge of the situation, and not the teacher. You can find some age-specific strategies for gaining silence and attention in chapters 13 and 14. Here are a few general approaches for you to try:

- *The force of your personality:* If you are teaching a reasonably well-behaved class, simply standing with your arms folded and looking mean can work. Hold your nerve and refuse to begin teaching until there is silence. You will find that, within a couple of minutes, many classes will fall silent of their own accord.
- *The power of the pause:* When you are in the middle of talking to the class, and an individual begins to talk, use a pause to indicate that you are waiting for silence. At first it can feel as though you are wasting lots of time, but eventually you will train your students in the expected behaviour.
- *Visual cues:* Add an interesting visual element to your pauses by using an egg timer. Every time you have to wait for the class, turn the timer over so that some sand runs through. Once the children fall silent, turn the egg timer on its side so that the sand remains in place. This gives a visual indication of

how much time the class has wasted, and how much time they will have to earn back (either through good work/ behaviour, or perhaps in a detention).

- *The non-verbal 'silence command':* In some subjects or situations, you may need to use an agreed signal to achieve silence. For instance, in PE or drama lessons, the students may be engaged in a noisy activity in an open space. In a nursery or reception aged class, the children might be engrossed in a game and less conscious of non-verbal signals. Train the class to respond quickly to your chosen signal, practising and praising the children until they react in the correct way. Here are some examples of 'silence commands':
  - A whistle or bell.
  - Rapping three times on a desk.
  - 'Hands up' – the teacher raises a hand and the children must stop what they are doing, put their hands up, and be silent.
  - The 'silent seat' – the teacher sits down in a designated seat, and the children must come to sit on the carpet in silence.
- *The well-chosen phrase:* With some classes a verbal cue for silence will work, although never shout over the students. If necessary, repeat the phrase several times over, pausing briefly to gauge the students' response. Try using some of the following phrases to gain silence:
  - 'I'd like you all to look this way and listen very carefully.'
  - 'Looking at me and listening please.'
  - 'I want complete silence before I continue.'
  - 'I want silence in five ... four ... three ... two ... one.'

In your first lesson with a class, talk to the students about why you have set this particular boundary, one that they *must* learn to follow. In addition to listening to you in silence, insist that they listen to each other in silence as well. You might like to talk with your children about why silence is important – here are some suggestions:

- so that the class can hear instructions;
- so that the students can learn effectively;
- to show respect for the teacher;

- to show respect for each other;
- because they would want others to listen silently to them;
- for their own safety (in case you need to give them an urgent command);
- because it's polite.

Make use of cues

A lot of teacher stress is caused by fairly low level misbehaviour – children calling out answers rather than putting their hands up, students going to start an activity before you have finished explaining it. The idea behind using cues is to cue the children into the behaviour you *do* want, rather than letting them behave incorrectly first, then having to tell them off. You can use cues for any behaviour that is repeated regularly, and they can be verbal or non-verbal. Cues will often change over time – gradually turning into a form of shorthand understood by both teacher and children. Here are a couple of examples to show you what I mean:

- *Answering questions:* Start any whole-class question with the phrase 'Put your hand up if you can tell me . . .'. By specifying the behaviour you want (hands up), you should anticipate and overcome the incorrect response (calling out). This instruction might be gradually abbreviated to 'Hands up' or simply 'Hands!' Eventually, it might be replaced by the teacher slightly raising a hand if a child goes to call out.
- *Giving instructions:* Some keen students will want to start work before you have even finished giving instructions. Use the phrase 'When I say go I want you to start . . .'. Once you have finished your explanation, set the class off to work by saying '3, 2, 1, go.' Again, this can become a shorthand, for instance with the teacher asking 'Did I say go?' when a child looks like starting work early.

Give them 'the choice'

We cannot actually *force* our children to behave – we can only make it seem like the best of all possible options. Ideally, we want our students to take responsibility for their own actions, and for the consequences of those actions. This is important in creating a positive and effective environment for learning. It is also vital in setting young people up for their lives beyond school, when the choices they make about behaviour become potentially that much more crucial ('Should I go with my friends to burgle that house or not?').

This is where the technique of 'the choice' comes in. Children essentially have two choices in the classroom: either they do as the teacher asks, or they accept the consequences of a refusal to comply. If we make the choices and consequences simple and clear enough, this can often prevent misbehaviour from occurring or escalating. It also encourages students to consider and change their negative behaviours, to avoid the unwelcome consequences in the future.

Where a teacher uses 'the choice', it can help to depersonalize a whole range of tricky situations. What you are effectively saying is that you are responsible for enforcing the rules specified by the school. If a student refuses to comply, he or she is making you apply the relevant consequences, rather than it being your own decision to give a punishment. When using 'the choice':

- state the behaviour you require;
- make clear the positive benefits of doing as you ask;
- make clear the consequences of refusing to comply;
- give the student a short time to consider his or her decision;
- if the student decides not to comply, apply the sanctions you have specified.

Here are a couple of examples of a teacher using 'the choice', to show you how it works:

Low-level disruption

Navdeep is playing with a Gameboy below the desk.

Teacher: Put the Gameboy away right now, please Navdeep, so that you can get on with your work.
Navdeep: Let me just finish this game, please Miss?
Teacher: Navdeep, you have a choice. I want you to put the gameboy away right now, or you will force me to confiscate it. It's up to you to decide. I'll come back to check on you in a moment.

The teacher bends down to help the student next to Navdeep. Navdeep sheepishly puts the gameboy away.

The serious incident

Sandra is in a terrible mood. As she enters the classroom, she shoves her way past a group of girls, pushing one student to the floor.

Teacher: [*pointing to the door*] Sandra! That is unacceptable behaviour. I want you to come outside with me right now, please, so we can discuss this.
Sandra: Nah, I won't. Are you gonna make me?
Teacher: Sandra. You have a choice. I want you to come outside with me right now so we can sort this out. If you refuse, I will have to send for a senior teacher to remove you from my lesson, and I really don't want to do that. I'll wait for you outside while you make your decision.

Realizing she has no way to win, Sandra follows the teacher outside.

Be reasonable, but don't reason with them

I was given this tip by a headteacher in a Scottish school, and it struck me as a wonderful summary of an effective and balanced approach to behaviour management. So long as you are reasonable with your students, and you don't have unrealistic expectations about how they will work or behave, then there is no need to actually reason with them over what you do ask them to do.

On a whole-class level, it is entirely reasonable to demand complete silence from the class while you explain the work, *so long as* you don't then proceed to talk at them for twenty minutes at a time. Similarly, it is reasonable to ask for written work to be done in silence, *so long as* you don't expect the students to work silently for an entire lesson without any breaks.

When individual misbehaviour is challenged, a child will often try to drag the teacher into a discussion, rather than accepting responsibility for what has happened. Some students are very clever at deflecting the teacher's challenge, and it is important to learn to stick to your guns, rather than be drawn into endless debates about 'whose fault it was'. For instance, you notice that a child is not doing any work. As soon as you challenge him, he blames another student for stealing his pen. You are then dragged into a discussion with this other child, who denies responsibility. Before you know it, you have forgotten all about the original misbehaviour you had planned to challenge.

The 'being reasonable' part of the equation can prove tricky for teachers to manage. We need to make difficult decisions about the right balance to strike. While we want to set high standards, and to expect the very best from all our students, we must maintain a sense of what is realistic. When teachers are too authoritarian with their demands, confrontations and difficulties can arise. Similarly, when teachers are too reasonable and relaxed, students will probably take advantage.

Use statements, not questions

Teachers can be particularly guilty of using rhetorical questions when managing behaviour – I know that I fall into this trap myself. It's the classic scenario: a student calls you a 'f*****g b*****d' and your response is 'What did you say?' At which point, the student answers your question by repeating the insult. I suspect it might be a matter of habit – because we frequently use lots of questions in our everyday teaching, we get used to this kind of vocal style. To help you overcome the habit, a really useful rule of thumb is 'never ask a question if you don't want to get an answer'.

The best approach is for the teacher to use statements of what is required, rather than questions about what isn't. This approach is much more helpful to the students – you state what they should be doing, rather than complaining about what they are not. It also gives the impression of a teacher who knows what he or she wants, and has confidence that the children will comply. Of course, in some situations a question will be appropriate and you will want to receive an answer. For instance, asking a child, 'Is there something the matter today?' might be a good starting point for a discussion about misbehaviour.

Here are a few examples of questions, and how they might be rephrased as statements, to show you what I mean:

- 'Why aren't you doing the work?' becomes 'I want you to get on with the work now, so that you can leave on time.'
- 'Why are you being so silly?' becomes 'I want you to sit properly in your chair and focus on the lesson, please.'
- 'Why aren't you listening?' becomes 'Everyone looking this way and listening in silence, please.'

Use repetition

Much of the time, when we say something in the classroom, we expect it to be heard and understood the first time around. This is not necessarily a sensible expectation to have, and it may lead to unnecessary misunderstandings and confrontations. Classrooms can be noisy and confusing places for our students: there might be many different reasons why your children do not respond immediately to your directions. Here are some of the times when you might usefully use repetition:

- To get a student's attention before you give an instruction.
- To ensure a child is listening when you need to warn him or her about a potential sanction.
- Because your students might not hear your instructions the first time you give them.
- To clarify any possible misunderstandings and make your wishes perfectly clear.
- In order to reinforce your instructions and make it clear that they must be followed.

Repetition is particularly helpful when you have to sanction a student. In this situation, you might repeat:

- The name of the student, to get his or her attention.
- The instruction you have given or the behaviour you do want. (You could ask the student to repeat this, to check for understanding.)
- The options for avoiding a sanction.
- The sanction you are imposing, if the child fails to comply.

Here is a specific example of how you might use repetition during an incident of misbehaviour. In this example, Adrian is chatting to his friends rather than doing his work.

Teacher: Adrian.

The teacher waits, there is no response.

Teacher: Adrian. I'd like you to look at me and listen.
Adrian: What, Miss?

He is still looking at his friends.

Teacher: Adrian. I said I'd like you to look at me and listen, please.

Finally, he turns around and looks at the teacher.

Teacher: Thank you, Adrian. Right, I want you to get on with your work right now. No more talking please.
Adrian: OK then.

He turns back, but continues chatting.

Teacher: Oh Adrian?
Adrian: Yeah?
Teacher: Could you repeat what I just said? What was my instruction?
Adrian: To get on with my work and stop talking.
Teacher: Good. I'm glad you understand. I'd hate to have to give you a detention, but I will if you don't stop chatting and get on with your work.

Set targets and time limits

Children love to have clear objectives – to be given a specific target at which to aim. Targets can help you harness your children's natural sense of competition: perhaps against other students in the class, but more importantly against their own previous levels of achievement. Having a clear amount to achieve, within a set time frame, helps create a sense of urgency and pace to the work. It gives a clear structure – something definite towards which the students can work. Targets can also help your less able children feel a sense of achievement – where a teacher asks the students to brainstorm five words in three minutes, even the least able should be able to complete this task.

There are a whole range of different targets that you might use. You might set a target for how many words or answers the children must complete. You could set a time for completing the work. You might give a target for improving behaviour, such as staying in seats, or putting up hands. When setting targets, use the following tips to help you get it right:

- Make sure your targets suit the class and the children: don't make them impossibly hard to achieve, nor conversely too easy.

- Keep your targets short and specific for maximum impact – five words, three minutes, and so on.
- Add visual prompts to aid understanding, for instance holding up a hand to show 'five words'.
- Use music to help create a sense of pace and urgency, for instance the theme tune from *Mission Impossible*.
- Use language to enhance your students' motivation levels: words such as 'competition', 'prize' and 'challenge'.
- Make sure any rewards offered for completion of targets are ones that really appeal to the class or the child.

To illustrate this technique further, here are some examples of a teacher setting targets:

A whole-class target for work

'Right. Today we're going to have a competition. As you can see, I've written ten questions up on the board about the work we did last lesson. The first person to answer all ten, in full sentences, can leave first when the bell goes. Ready, steady, go!'

An individual target for work

'OK, Arwel. What I want you to do today is to concentrate on putting full stops in your writing, but they must be in the right place. Don't worry too much about spelling, because today we're going to focus on the punctuation. And if you do manage to put all the full stops in, you can choose one of these fantastic stickers.'

A whole-class target for behaviour

'Right, class, looking this way and listening very carefully please. That's superb. Today we're going to have a test. [Groans from the class.] *No! Not that kind of test. This is a test to see who has the best self-discipline in the class. And there's a very special prize for the winner. I want to see who can work in silence for the longest time, and the best person gets to eat this chocolate bar in front of the whole class!'*

An individual target for behaviour

'Now then, Chris, I know how hard you find it to stay in your seat, so today I'm going to set you a challenge. If you can stay in your chair for the whole lesson, without getting up once, you can win three whole merits. I'll give you one merit for every twenty minutes that you manage to sit still. OK?'

Use *humour*

Humour is incredibly powerful in the classroom. Teachers who make their students laugh, and who can laugh with them when appropriate, will inevitably form good relationships with their classes. Of course there will be times when you can't see the funny side. On a Monday morning/Friday afternoon, when you're tired, hungover, full of cold or just plain cranky, you might not feel in the mood for a stand-up comedy routine. But if you can take a fun approach to the job, and make the work and the lessons seem like light relief, this will definitely help you in managing behaviour.

Alongside its beneficial effects on students, humour also offers a respite from the tension that may build up in a poorly behaved class. If you can learn to laugh when things go wrong, or to make your teaching fun for yourself, you will feel a whole lot better. You will also help yourself avoid the defensiveness that can occur in confrontational situations, and you will be much more relaxed in dealing with any problems that do arise.

You can use humour to dissipate the threat of a personal insult, by simply agreeing with what the student has said to you. Hard as it is to react calmly when you are feeling hurt or offended, this technique turns the insult around by refusing to acknowledge its impact. So, when a student says, 'Your hair looks really stupid like that, Miss', you could simply answer in a deadpan voice, 'Yes, I know, and I'm going to sue my hairdresser.'

Learn to laugh at yourself when you make a mistake in your

classroom, for instance tripping over a wire or saying something stupid. Children seem to really welcome a teacher who has the ability to be self-deprecating. It's a good way of undermining the image of teacher as authoritarian figure, and it shows that you don't take yourself too seriously.

Generally speaking, it is best to avoid sarcasm, although I do appreciate that it can offer a great way of letting off steam in really difficult situations. You should also avoid laughing at, and encouraging other children to laugh at, individual students. Your 'class clowns' might enjoy the attention, but some shy children may be mortified to hear their peers laughing at them.

Put yourself in their shoes

When you have to deal with persistent misbehaviour, it can be easy to lose your sense of perspective. You might begin to feel that the students are deliberately being awkward, and that they have a personal vendetta against you. In turn, this can lead to overreactions to what is in fact relatively minor misbehaviour. Develop the ability to step outside yourself, and to view what happens in your classroom from the children's perspective. Become a reflective and self-analytical teacher, and this will feed into every aspect of your practice.

Putting yourself in your children's shoes is a useful technique when an activity or a whole lesson doesn't seem to be working. By viewing the situation from the perspective of your class, you should be able to discover what it is about the work that is leading to poor behaviour. Is there too much listening and not enough doing? Is the concept too hard for the class to grasp? Or do the students simply find this particular topic area boring?

Similarly, you can analyse your own teaching by using this approach. If your children become confrontational with you when you try to discipline them, step back and view the way that you deal with the behaviour from the outside. Are you saying or doing something which is exacerbating the situation? Are there some external factors, such as time of day, at work?

When you take on the adult role of 'teacher', make sure that you don't lose sight of what it was like to be a child. Sometimes children will simply be messing around because they are children. Winding up teachers has been a classic childhood pursuit since schools were first invented!

Part Two

THE TEACHER
AND THE
TEACHING

4

THE EFFECTIVE
TEACHER

The learning process

Becoming an effective teacher is a learning process that starts the first time you set foot in a classroom, and is one that should never really end, no matter how many years of experience you have in the job. There are many different facets to the effective teacher – skilled verbal and non-verbal communication, the ability to manage the class and the classroom space, an understanding of how to match teaching style to a particular situation, the knowledge to plan for and deliver high quality lessons. All of these qualities can be learned and developed, and each of us will benefit from working on particular areas of our own practice. In this chapter I look at those aspects of effective teaching that are connected to the teacher as a person and a communicator, rather than as an educator. (See Chapter 7 for advice on planning and delivering the curriculum.)

It's probably fair to say that some people are born teachers – they seem to have a natural ability to engage with and inspire children, to transmit ideas or knowledge, and to control the behaviour of groups of people. To an extent, this is about charisma, self-confidence and the power of personality. For these natural teachers, the skills and attitudes described in this chapter might come instinctively. But we can't all be born teachers, and in any case it's the willingness to learn and develop that is important, and not the point from which you start that process.

The teacher as role model

At first, the idea of being a role model can take a bit of getting used to. Sometimes you will be a role model simply by virtue of your age, gender, subject area or social/cultural background. You might be the only male working-class teacher working in your primary school, or the only black female physics teacher in your local area. But the teacher as role model is about much more than that. It's about providing a consistent model of appropriate behaviour and attitudes, often for children who lack this model outside of the school environment. Some of our most difficult students will be used to adults behaving in an aggressive or immature way: it can take time for them to realize that there are other ways of interacting with the world.

Children model what they see, and it is worth keeping this in mind when you are frustrated by the behaviour of some of your students. If a child has been brought up in a house where every other word is a swear word, then it is likely that he or she will bring this language into school. But if they respect you, your students will want to emulate you. They might model your behaviour and your ways of relating to people; they might study the subject you teach to A level and beyond, because you have inspired them to love it as much as you do.

One of the key ways we can model good behaviour for our students is to treat them as we would wish to be treated ourselves, i.e. politely and with respect. We might like to think that being polite would be a relatively straightforward strategy to adopt and maintain. However, when faced with the stress caused by persistent aggression or rudeness from students, it is all too easy to get sucked into a similar attitude. Before you know it, you are making rude comments and being sarcastic – something you would probably never do in your life outside of school.

It can be hard but, if you can achieve it, a relentlessly polite manner will help you defuse difficult situations and set an appropriate example of good behaviour. When disciplining recalcitrant students, always remember that the rest of your class are watching and learning from you. If they see you remaining calm and polite whatever the provocation, they will see that your approach is right and that the student who misbehaves is wrong.

The examples below show the teacher offering two very different models of behaviour. In the first instance, notice how the comments very quickly become a 'tit-for-tat' battle of rudeness. In the second scenario, you can see the teacher staying relaxed and defusing every rude comment that Jackie makes.

Reacting 'in kind'

Teacher: Jackie, get on with your work and stop causing problems.
Jackie: No I won't. This work is stupid and your lessons are boring!
Teacher: No, Jackie, you're stupid and boring, not the work.
Jackie: Don't you call me stupid and boring, you old cow.
Teacher: How dare you call me an old cow! Right, you're in detention.
Jackie: Oh yeah? Well I'm not staying behind with *you*. I hate you.
Teacher: And I hate you too. [*shouting*] NOW GET ON WITH THE WORK!

Modelling polite behaviour

Teacher: Jackie, please could you get on with your work now.
Jackie: No I won't. This work is stupid and your lessons are boring!
Teacher: I'm very sorry that you feel like that. Now please do the work.
Jackie: No I won't! You're an old cow!
Teacher: Well, I might be a *cow*, but I'm not that old, am I, Jackie?
Jackie: [*totally confused by this response*] What?
Teacher: Now please get on with the work. You have ten minutes to finish and I'd love to see how well you can do.

Effective verbal and non-verbal communication

When you step in front of a class, you take on a role or character to communicate with your audience, just as an actor does when he or she walks out onto the stage. Your children will be taking their cues about how to behave at least partly from the way that you use your voice and your body. Where teachers communicate confidence and certainty, this helps them to achieve a high level of status. The students look up to them, respect them, and consequently behave for them.

It is important to think carefully about the physical aspects of your teaching, particularly if you are not naturally a confident person. Remember that you don't have to feel confident inside, you just need to communicate a confident persona through your verbal and non-verbal signals. Right from the start, your children will be examining your teacher persona (often subconsciously), to decide how they are going to behave.

Using your voice

The teacher's voice is a tool, an instrument that must be used every single day of our working lives. It is vital that we learn to take good care of our vocal instruments – we only have one and we cannot send it away to be repaired. Some teachers will have been trained in good vocal technique, but it is still easy to pick up bad habits along the way. Make sure that you maintain good posture when speaking – standing upright with your shoulders, neck and chin relaxed. Aim to use your diaphragm to create vocal sounds, rather than the muscles in and around your neck. If you are unsure about good voice usage, or if you regularly lose your voice, ask your school to send you for some training.

Your voice says a lot about you to your classes: it will have a powerful impact on your children, and on their perceptions of you. We all have our own vocal 'style' or personality, which says a lot about us as individuals. Think for a moment about the voices of some high-profile figures: where a vocal sound grates or irritates you, this can make you feel negative about the person generally. On the other hand, a beautiful speaking or singing voice can help create a positive feeling about someone.

The sound of your voice will give other people lots of clues about how you are feeling. When faced with a stressful situation, our voices can very easily betray our emotions, becoming louder, or cracking under pressure. Your voice gives your students a very clear indication of your inner state, and they will respond to the signals given through the way that you talk. The secret is for you to be in control: if you need to change the sound of your voice, this should be a conscious decision, rather than being done as a result of stress. You might be feeling angry and bad tempered, but you can still make your voice sound calm and controlled.

While you don't necessarily want to completely change the way that you speak between the normal world and the classroom, it is important to understand the way that your voice can impact on your ability to manage behaviour. High quality verbal communication will help you develop good relationships with your children, it will encourage them to behave better, and it will also protect your voice. Below are lots of tips and suggestions about using your voice more effectively.

Volume

It can be very difficult for teachers to achieve and sustain good volume levels. Although we might hope that we could just 'talk normally' to our students, all the stresses and strains of the typical classroom situation mean that this is often hard to maintain. Getting the right balance in your volume levels is very important in managing behaviour. It helps you show respect for your students and emotional self-control; it also helps you teach in a way that ensures understanding.

Shouting usually indicates a loss of emotional control – something that some students enjoy seeing in their teachers. This can be extremely damaging for your voice, and it rarely has any direct impact on misbehaviour. It also signals an 'old school', authoritarian approach that seems out of sync with modern approaches to education. Remember, too, that some children (typically the well-behaved ones whom you want to encourage) may feel very scared if you shout at them.

Here are some suggestions to help you get volume levels right, and avoid the urge to shout.

- Remember – the quieter you are as a teacher, the quieter your classes will have to be to hear you. Don't overdo it and whisper, though, as a forced whisper can hurt your voice.

- Aim for a conversational volume level, and be constantly aware of how your emotional state is affecting the sound of your voice.
- If you feel yourself getting wound up, pause for a few seconds to regain self-control, before you continue to speak. Breathe deeply and deliberately lower your volume levels.
- Learn to 'throw' your voice like an actor to an audience. Imagine the sound as a physical entity – a stone for example – and 'throw' it out towards the class or the individual.
- Talking loudly can become a matter of habit. Listen to yourself regularly during your lessons, doing a mental check on whether you are speaking at an appropriate volume level.
- When bringing down the volume level in your lessons, imagine turning down the sound on a stereo. Try lowering the sound by about half – you may be surprised just how quietly you can talk and still be heard.
- Take acoustics into account. If you teach in different rooms, learn to adapt volume levels for the relevant room. Typically, the empty space in halls and gyms will make your voice echo, while a crowded classroom can muffle the sound.
- When you have to talk to an individual about his or her behaviour, get close to the student and talk quietly, so that no one else can hear.
- Sometimes, raising your voice can provide a useful short, sharp shock for a lively or talkative class.
- If the teacher makes a conscious decision to raise his or her voice, this can be done from a position of emotional control, rather than as an angry and instinctive reaction.
- Where the teacher retains self-control, this will help with vocal technique: the sound will tend to come from the diaphragm muscles rather than from tension in the throat.

Tone

Tone is very useful for giving interest and excitement to your teaching. It also helps you create a sense of engagement with your students, because it gives them clues and cues about your emotional state. There are many subtle ways in which we can adapt and vary our teacher 'characters' by making use of different tones. A wide range of tones will help us signal a whole range of thoughts, feelings, reactions and responses to the children.

The more use you make of tone, the more you will tend to use your face and your body as you teach. A deadpan voice gives a feeling of disengagement and a flat or lifeless facial expression. If a teacher speaks entirely without tone, then it won't be long before the children get bored and misbehave. On the other hand an animated voice, full of tone, will light up the face, eyes and body and create a sense of connection.

Generally speaking, the younger the children you teach, the more tone you should put into your voice. If you teach students whose first language is not English, then an over-exaggerated tone, with lots of emphasis, will help them understand what you are saying. Bear in mind that with some older, cynical or demotivated students, excessive use of tone might be interpreted as patronizing.

There are various tones that can be particularly useful to the teacher, and some of these are detailed below.

- *Wonder:* Putting a tone of wonder and interest into your voice will help you engage a class. You might also use this tone when you are particularly pleased with a child's behaviour: 'Oh! I'm so pleased with how you've done today.'
- *Excitement:* An excited tone can help you give pace and energy to a subject or activity. It can help you motivate and inspire children to participate fully in the learning.
- *Deadly:* This is a tone that tells your students that you are *not* happy, and it can helpfully be used alongside the 'deadly stare' (see below, 'Using your body'). It is a cold, calculated sound, rather than one of anger.
- *Disappointed:* When dealing with misbehaviour, disappointment is one of the most valuable tones of all. Where the class or student respects the teacher, the sense that 'you've let me down' is a very powerful motivator to improve.

Pace

Pace is a very interesting and subtle area of voice usage. Different teachers will have their own 'styles' when it comes to the speed at which they like to speak. It's important to adapt the pace you use according to the students you are teaching. With young children, or with those whose language or cognitive skills are not well developed, you will need to speak slowly and clearly. On the other hand, with a class who are cynical and disengaged with learning, you might need to 'gee them up' by using a fast pace, to get and keep their interest.

Try to use a good range of different paces during a lesson as this will help you add interest to the learning. It's a question of balance: keep your children engaged but ensure that everyone can understand what you are saying. Here are some thoughts about how a slow or fast pace might help or hinder you in managing behaviour and learning.

A slow pace can:

- Calm a student down;
- Relax a tense situation;
- Quieten a noisy or overexcited class;
- Help ensure understanding.

But it can also:

- Lead to boredom;
- Encourage students to switch off;
- Be perceived as patronizing;
- Make the teacher appear pompous.

A fast pace can:

- Motivate a disengaged class;
- Perk up a lazy child;
- Give a lesson energy and forward momentum;
- Add interest to a dull area of the curriculum.

But it can also:

- Hamper proper understanding;
- Make some children feel stressed;
- Make the teacher sound harassed;
- Be wearing on the teacher.

Teacher talk

While on the subject of voice usage, it is worth considering how much you should actually talk at all. Teachers are a bit notorious for loving the sound of their own voices. I know that I personally can be guilty of talking at my students far too much and for far too long. When you speak at a class for more than about five or ten minutes, it is likely that at least some of your students will have phased out the sound of your voice, and will be contemplating misbehaviour. As far as possible, keep teacher talk to a minimum and active student learning to a maximum.

Listening to someone talk is typically a very passive activity, so when you do have to talk for longer periods, find ways to keep your students involved. Intersperse your speaking with exercises that require the children to actually do something. For instance, you might ask them to:

- Make notes;
- Pick out key words;
- Draw diagrams;
- Look at a visual aid;
- Answer questions;
- Help you do some demonstrations.

Using your body

There are a whole host of non-verbal signals that teachers give which have an impact on student behaviour. Of course, some of these signals we use very consciously, to help us control our classes. But we will also be giving many subconscious signals at the same time, ones that can betray a lack of confidence or a sense of stress. The way that our students interpret these signals can help or hinder us in managing behaviour. Much of the time, your children will be taking decisions about how to behave based on a subconscious reading of what you are 'saying' with your body. As with your voice, the secret is to become aware of the signals you send, and to stay in control of these signals as far as is humanly possible.

It can be tempting to use mainly spoken instructions and signals to put across your wishes and instructions to a class. However, there are some good reasons why non-verbal signals are more useful and powerful than spoken ones.

- They send a very powerful message of control and status to the students: 'I can get you to do what I want, apparently without saying anything at all!'
- They require very little effort from the teacher, and they do not put a strain on your voice.
- They can be used on individuals, without alerting the rest of the class to what is going on, and consequently preventing the attention seeker from gaining an audience.
- Over time, these signals will be turned into a kind of non-verbal 'shorthand' that you can use to 'talk' to your class.

Your whole body can play a part in communicating with your students – from the face right down to the feet. Below you can find advice about making effective use of the various parts of your body. I have also devoted a separate section to ideas on how the teacher might best use the classroom space.

The eyes and eyebrows

When you're addressing the class, keep your eyes moving around, checking that all the faces are staring right back at you. If they're not, wait. Remember: never, ever talk until you have *everyone's* attention. By using your eyes to scan around the classroom during your lessons, you might catch an incident of misbehaviour before it starts, and be able to nip it in the bud.

61

The 'deadly stare' can be an extremely effective non-verbal signal. Behind the deadly stare is the knowledge (or at least the pretence) that you 'know what you want' and you 'know what will happen if you don't get what you want' (see Chapter 1). If you can achieve this mental attitude, or at least give the impression you feel this way, your eyes will communicate your deadly state of mind.

The deadly stare is difficult to describe, but you will certainly know when you have mastered it. It tells your students that they must do what you want, or they are likely to suffer the ghastly consequences, something that is clearly *not* recommended. Take care not to let your deadly stare move outside of the confines of the school and into your normal life – watch that you don't experiment with it on family or friends, or on tubes and buses.

Raising your eyebrows is a good way of expressing surprise or disapproval. Some lucky teachers are able to raise a single eyebrow to say: 'Excuse me, exactly *what* do you think you are doing?' Your students will quickly get used to seeing you use your eyes to give non-verbal signals. When a class is not paying attention, try taking away eye contact from the class and looking instead at the ceiling. Where the teacher normally makes constant eye contact, this removal clearly indicates 'I'm waiting'.

The face

Your students spend a fair amount of time looking at your face. If they see that it is constantly moving, smiling and relaxed, but always alert, then they will believe that you are in charge. Your face will also betray any tension or defensiveness you feel, so make a conscious effort to keep your expressions cool and calm.

The hands

Our hands can be incredibly expressive – we can 'talk' with them to our students almost as readily as we can with our voices. A teacher who uses his or her hands as a natural part of the teaching process will tend to engage the children and create a feeling of inclusiveness. Many hand signals can become part of your 'shorthand' with the class – you can quickly tell them what you want from them without needing to speak. Avoid pointing at children who are misbehaving: it can create a negative reaction, as it singles out an individual in an aggressive way.

There are a whole host of positive hand signals that you might use. You could:

- Put a finger to your lips to indicate that the class should be silent;
- Tug on your ear to show that the children must listen;
- Click to gain an individual's attention;
- Place your hand on the desk of a child who is misbehaving;
- Hold one hand out, palm outwards, to say 'stop!';
- Put your hands out, palms gently pushing downwards, to suggest that the children should calm themselves down.

The body: stance

The stance that you take with your body will communicate a great deal to the class, as will your overall posture. Aim to look confident – standing tall and keeping your body open and relaxed. Use different positions to indicate your wishes. For instance, standing with your arms folded when you are waiting to begin the lesson suggests that you will not start teaching until the class do as you wish. Standing with hands on hips gives a slightly more assertive signal when a class is misbehaving.

The body: actions and non-actions

As the saying goes, 'actions speak louder than words', and teachers will often develop a whole repertoire of different actions to talk with their children. You might look pointedly at your watch, to indicate that a class is wasting (their own) time. You could write down a child's name during an incident of misbehaviour – this will often cause them to stop and check what you are doing and why.

Refusing to take any action at all can send as powerful a non-verbal signal as doing something. For instance, you might call the class's bluff and simply stand waiting for silence, refusing to start work until the children cooperate. This sends an incredibly clear signal about your expectations and intentions.

The body: levels

If the teacher always stands upright, and above the students, he or she is communicating a subtle message of superiority over them. Although you want to be in *control* of the situation, this is not the same as suggesting that you are somehow more important than the students. Varying your body levels shows your students that you are extremely confident about your ability to keep control. It also says that you respect them enough to come down to their level, both literally and metaphorically.

Changing your height level in relation to a student can send a whole range of different signals. Crouching down beside a child lessens the perceived sense of authority or intimidation. It also helps you communicate much more effectively on a one-to-one basis, keeping the interaction private.

Putting yourself in a position which is actually lower than the students (e.g. sitting on the floor) can offer a useful element of surprise. Similarly, I find that occasionally sitting or even standing on a desk can create an interesting shift in perspective.

The body: appearance

Although it might not be politically correct to admit it, it is inevitable that your students will be making some judgements about you based on how you look. Barring cosmetic surgery, there's not an awful lot you can do about your overall appearance. In any case, it is not so much a matter of whether you are good-looking or ugly, fat or thin, but more about how you express your inner sense of self through the way that you look.

Being smartly turned out tends to make a good impression with students, because it suggests that you take yourself and your work seriously. On the other hand, some teachers can get away with being scruffy and unconventional looking, because of the power of their personalities. In some school situations, wearing a smart suit will help you reinforce an air of authority. Similarly, some subjects will lend themselves to more casual or creative clothing than others.

The teacher within the space

The way that you use your teaching space communicates a complex non-verbal message about your style, and about whether you are in control. When we feel defensive, it is tempting to back into a corner, perhaps up against the white-board, a place of safety. Unfortunately, the rebels usually formulate their plans for trouble in the back row of the classroom. And if you're stuck at the front you won't be able to deal with them. Here are some suggestions for using the space to give positive non-verbal signals.

- *Stand proud:* No matter how bad you are feeling, try not to let your body show it. Even when the class is rioting, stand up straight and proud, and give off an air of confidence.
- *Mark your territory:* As far as your energy levels allow, keep moving around the teaching space. This applies when the students are at work on an activity, but it can also be done while you are explaining the lesson. Doing this will:
  - Help mark the space as 'yours' – showing you as in control of the entire space;
  - Keep your students on their toes, because they will never know when you might be approaching from behind;
  - Ensure that you 'visit' every child during the course of each lesson;
  - Help you view the classroom and the students from a range of perspectives.
- *Get close to the troublemakers:* When we are plotting trouble, the last thing that we want is for someone to find out. Get in close proximity to the troublemakers in your class, so that you can stamp out any trouble before it takes hold. There is normally no need to actually say anything – the child quickly becomes

uncomfortable about messing around with a teacher standing close by.
- *Give 'em a shock:* Sometimes it can be useful to suddenly change the spatial aspects of your style or your teaching space. This might mean rearranging the classroom from groups of desks to rows; clearing the desks away and asking the class to sit on the floor; or even completely turning around all the desks to face in the opposite direction. Rearranging the space helps the students take a fresh perspective on what happens in the room.

Psychological aspects of teaching

Of course, effective teaching is not solely about the physical aspects of verbal and non-verbal communication. There are also various psychological approaches that you can use to help you manage behaviour. This is as much about keeping yourself in a positive frame of mind as it is about keeping control over your class. Ideally, you should feel calm, relaxed, but alert. Below are a few suggestions as to how you might achieve this state of mind.

- *Keep 'em guessing:* Although I have stressed the importance of consistency with your students, it doesn't pay to be too predictable all the time. Sometimes (and do it sparingly) you could make a sudden change in your teaching style. Perhaps you are normally quiet and firm. Once in a while, show them that you have another, louder and sharper side to you.
- *Turn on a penny:* Similarly, sometimes you might make a sudden change in your entire manner if you feel it is necessary. For instance, you might be having a really good lesson, when Jack decides to spoil things by messing around. It could prove very effective to suddenly turn to him, say viciously, *'How dare you spoil this lesson for my wonderful class!'* and then become 'sweetness and light' again.
- *Convince yourself:* If you can convince yourself, *really* convince yourself, that you are in charge, then you will appear to be so. If you truly know where you're coming from (are aware) and

exactly what you want (are definite) then the psychological battle is practically won.

- *Maintain a psychological distance:* Although it can be hard, do learn to keep an emotional distance from the misbehaviour that you encounter. Refuse to become emotionally involved with incidents of poor behaviour and this will help you retain a sense of distance and a feeling of control.
- *Don't take it personally.* Rather than viewing poor behaviour as an attack on you, it is far more effective and meaningful to take a sympathetic view. Remind yourself that children who misbehave generally have some sort of problem of their own. And at the end of the day, no matter how badly behaved your classes are, it really is not the end of the world.

5

TEACHING
STYLES

What is a teaching style?

There are of course as many styles of teaching as there are teachers, because we are all individuals who work in our own unique ways. There are many facets that go together to make up a teaching style: your personality, the way you look, the way you speak, the way you use movement and space, the levels of control you use; in fact everything you do in the classroom (and beyond) will add to your own personal teaching style.

Each teacher's style will be developed over the course of time. When you first start out in the classroom, you may well use a style that suggests uncertainty or a lack of confidence. Unless you are hugely self-assured, this is almost inevitable. You need a chance to experiment, to make mistakes and to find your feet. It's worth remembering that you don't have to be the same person as a teacher that you are outside the classroom. You can put on a confident and outgoing teacher 'character', even if you feel shy and insecure inside. It is as much about student perception as it is about the reality of the situation.

Whatever style you end up using, there are certain aspects and approaches that will help you best manage your students' behaviour. You can make a conscious decision to incorporate these strategies into your style, to assist you in controlling your children's behaviour. An effective teaching style will show your class that *you* are in charge, but in a positive, respectful and humanitarian way.

Developing an assertive teaching style

Teaching styles typically fall somewhere along the line between passive, assertive and aggressive, with an assertive style being the ideal approach for effective behaviour management. It's well worth having an understanding of the elements of these different approaches, so that you can get as close as possible to the right balance in your own teaching. Some of us will lean naturally towards an aggressive, authoritarian teaching style, and might need to curb our instinctive tendency to get wound up and to overreact. Similarly, some of us will tend more towards a passive and defensive approach, and might need to build up our confidence and self-belief.

The conditions in which you work may well have an impact on the style that you adopt. If you teach in a situation where there is much difficult behaviour, you might constantly feel 'under attack' from the students. In these circumstances, it can be difficult not to 'fight back' by becoming equally aggressive. However, the more challenging the children, the more likely they are to react badly to an overly aggressive teaching style. In an 'easy' school (if there is such a thing!), you might tend towards over-passivity, allowing the students to take too much control of your classroom.

Below you can find some descriptions of these three types of approach, and some thoughts on how you can achieve a positive, assertive style in your teaching.

A passive style

A passive style is characterized by inactivity and defensiveness, and by an introverted and inward-looking approach. The teacher effectively hands over control of the classroom to the students. When managing behaviour, the teacher tends to use questions rather than statements, asking the students to do something rather than telling them. This lack of certainty means that it is not completely clear to the children what the teacher wishes them to do.

Here is an example of a classroom incident, played in a passive way:

Rob is holding a paper aeroplane and disrupting the class by threatening to throw it across the room.

Teacher: Rob, what are you doing with that?
Rob: Nothing.
Teacher: Are you sure you're not doing anything?
Rob: Of course I'm sure. [*He throws the plane.*]
Teacher: But you said you weren't doing anything!

An aggressive style

With an aggressive style, the teacher tends to come out of his or herself and at the students, often overreacting to minor misbehaviour. The teacher will typically be clear and definite about expected standards. However, these are applied without any recourse to reason or flexibility, and without any consideration of individual student needs.

The aggressive teacher tends to shout, using hostile body language and often being rude. This is very much the old-fashioned approach to teaching, in which the teacher acted as authoritarian figure, and the children were expected to do as they were told without any questions. Some teachers will use elements of this approach within their style (see the description of the 'strict and scary' teacher below). Where the students are willing to submit because of the teacher's personality or position of responsibility, this can keep a class under control. However, there is always the potential for a 'blow-up', as seen below. In addition, some quieter children might spend the lessons in a state of fear.

Rob is holding a paper aeroplane and disrupting the class by threatening to throw it across the room.

Teacher: [*shouting*] What on earth do you think you're doing? Give me that right now!
Rob: But sir, I was only ...
Teacher: Don't give me that rubbish. Are you stupid or something? Aeroplane. Give it to me. Now.
Rob: Don't shout at me.
Teacher: Don't tell me what to do, boy.
Rob: I'm not staying in your stupid lesson.
Teacher: How dare you call my lesson stupid!
Rob: I'm out of here. [*He storms out of the room.*]
Teacher: Where the hell do you think you're going?! You're in serious trouble now ...

An assertive style

Having an assertive teaching style is about asserting your control of the situation, while still being reasonable and polite over the demands that you make. The advice given throughout this book will help you develop a more assertive approach to your teaching. In general, you need to:

- Have clear and consistent expectations about behaviour and work;
- Be determined and certain that your students will live up to these expectations;
- Be flexible about your demands when the situation merits;
- Stay calm and polite at all times, and treat your students as you want them to treat you;
- Use deliberate statements of what you want to help you manage behaviour;
- Ask once nicely, then once firmly, then just get on with it!

Again, here is an example to demonstrate what I mean:

Rob is holding a paper aeroplane and disrupting the class by threatening to throw it across the room.

Teacher: Rob, give me that paper aeroplane right now please.
Rob: No.
Teacher: Rob, I want you to give me the paper aeroplane right now.
Rob: It's mine.
Teacher: Rob, if you continue to argue you will force me to put you in detention. [*Holds out hand.*] Give the paper aeroplane to me *now*.

Rob hands the paper aeroplane to the teacher.

Effective teaching styles

You will know yourself what kind of behaviour manager you can be. There is no point in trying to adopt a strict model with all your classes if you are small, petite, have a quiet voice, and hate shouting. On the other hand, you may be able to use the strict model to good effect in certain lessons. In fact, it can be more effective when a teacher who is normally reasonably quiet suddenly turns scary. This provides an excellent way of keeping your students on their toes.

In every school there is normally at least one teacher of whom the students feel a bit nervous or afraid. It's all part of the drama of school life. This teacher is often someone in a position of authority, because the higher up the ladder you go within a school, the more automatic respect you are normally given. In essence, this teacher can be strict without too much effort, often because of a prior reputation. Where it works, this 'strict and scary' style can be very effective, although it would not be my personal choice.

For the majority of us, the 'firm but fun' approach is the safest bet. This style closely models the assertive teaching style described above. It can be hard to establish a 'firm but fun' reputation for yourself, but once it is done you have the advantage of children who will do as you ask, but who also feel comfortable and happy in your company. You can find descriptions of these two different approaches below.

The 'strict and scary' teacher

Most of us know an example of this type of teacher: perhaps because we work with someone who adopts this approach, or maybe because we were taught by a strict and scary teacher ourselves when we were at school. Here are some of the characteristics of the strict and scary teacher:

- The demand is for perfect behaviour at all times.
- There is a high level of control over the students, for instance lining up in silence before entering the room, or working in complete silence during the lesson.

- There is little or no negotiation of rules or boundaries for behaviour with the class. What the teacher says, goes.
- The teacher will often shout at students when applying a sanction.
- Frequent use is made of sanctions to control the class.
- Sanctions are applied at the first sign of misbehaviour.

This particular teaching style has various advantages and disadvantages, both for the students and for the teacher using it:

Advantages:

- The students learn that they *must* behave, or they will be punished. It therefore becomes progressively easier to discipline them, once they understand the tight boundaries being imposed.
- The class is generally well disciplined, and a good deal of work takes place. Well-behaved students are not disrupted by their less well-behaved counterparts.
- The teacher does not have to strive to be in a good, fun mood all the time. The teacher can relieve some of his or her stress by shouting at the class.

Disadvantages:

- This style is physically tiring for the teacher. If a great deal of shouting goes on, the teacher's voice may become worn out or damaged.
- The teacher needs to be physically imposing for this style to work, or to have a strong 'presence'.
- Some of the quieter, well-behaved students can end up in a state of constant fear.
- There is less opportunity for explorative, creative, or group work, because the teacher needs to maintain silence for the style to be consistent.
- Although the students will behave for this type of teacher, they are unlikely to actually like him or her.
- There is more opportunity for serious confrontations to arise.

If a student decides to stand up to this type of teacher, it is almost impossible for the 'strict and scary' teacher to back down without losing face.

The 'firm but fun' teacher

This is what I personally would see as the ideal teacher/ behaviour manager. The firm but fun teacher is liked by the students, at the same time as having their respect. Here are some of the characteristics of this teacher:

- The teacher tells the class what is expected in terms of behaviour right from the start, and sticks to these rules consistently.
- There is some flexibility applied to rules on occasions where it seems appropriate.
- The teacher will raise his or her voice if necessary, but normally this is not required.
- The work is made interesting, and the students are set hard but achievable targets.
- The teacher focuses on positive methods of motivation, and uses more rewards than sanctions.
- When using sanctions, the teacher gives a series of warnings first.
- The teacher gets to know the students on a personal level.

This teaching style has the following advantages/disadvantages:

Advantages:

- The students learn to behave through the application of consistent boundaries. Once they have learned where the boundaries are, they will follow them without having to be told.
- The class is generally well disciplined, and a fair amount of work takes place.
- This style is more relaxed, and less stressful for both teacher and students. There is far less chance of confrontations arising.
- There is more opportunity for creative, exploratory work.

Disadvantages:

- There is a fine balance between being firm and being too relaxed with the class. If the line does slip in the wrong direction, it can be difficult to retrieve the situation.
- The teacher must be relentlessly consistent in applying the boundaries.
- The teacher must be in a good, fun mood for most or all of the time.
- Some of the less-well-behaved students may take advantage more easily.

Enhancing your teaching style

Of course there are many subtle variations in each individual teacher's personal style. Some will play the clown, using large splashes of humour to win over the children; others will take a very clear-cut, businesslike approach. Obviously it is wise to play up those parts of your personality that are going to appeal to the children, while playing down any more negative aspects. Here are some suggestions for refining and enhancing your teaching style beyond the more basic elements.

Buck the trend

Students can be quick to stereotype the kind of style they expect from a teacher, depending on the way that he or she appears. For instance, if you are a large, physically imposing, rugby-playing kind of bloke, then they will probably expect a 'strict and scary' approach from you. In fact, it can be very interesting to buck the stereotype and challenge their perceptions.

Be a 'real person'

It's quite a tricky balance to achieve between being viewed as a teacher figure and giving the students the sense that you are actually a human being as well. I have found that being self-deprecating works very well in achieving the 'real person' effect. When you make a mistake, be willing to admit it. Be brave enough to laugh at yourself if you say something stupid.

Don't try and be friends

A mistake that many new teachers make is to try and get friendly with their students, in the hope of keeping them on their side. I suspect this is particularly tempting if you are close in age to your students. Remember, though, that this will make it very hard to crack down on any boundary testing. Stay slightly removed from your students, no matter how well you get on with them as people.

Retain a 'mystique'

Although you want your students to see you as a real person, it is not a good idea to give too much of yourself away. After all, teaching is not your entire life, and it is psychologically beneficial to keep a part of yourself secret and separate from your work. In addition, cultivating a sense of mystery about yourself will make your students curious to find out more. Make it plain to your children that you have a full and interesting life outside of school, one that you wish to keep private. You could let slip brief hints about how exciting your private life is, while still retaining that crucial element of mystique.

Create a reputation

It is really rewarding to overhear students talking positively about your lessons with their peers. Word-of-mouth about a teacher can have a huge impact on student behaviour (for good or for bad!). Remember, our students do discuss us in the playground, just as we discuss them in the staffroom. There are a variety of ways that you can create and enhance your reputation:

- *Stay at a school for a long time:* As time goes by, your reputation (good, I hope) will precede you. Many schools take in younger brothers and sisters of those students who are already there.

And I can assure you, they will be discussing their teachers at home before they arrive.

- *Use an unusual lesson or lessons:* An inspiring lesson will influence the behaviour of your students for the better and it will also help you earn a good reputation.
- *Be an entertainer:* If your students view you as an entertaining, fun and interesting teacher, they will tell their peers all about you. When these students arrive at your lesson, at some point in the future, they will already have positive expectations.

Maintaining a positive approach

Never forget that teaching is not just about dealing with poorly behaved students; it is also about working with all those wonderfully well-behaved students as well. Too much focus on dealing with the difficult children can really slant your perspective, and also damage your prospects when it comes to managing behaviour. Aim to focus on the well-behaved students, getting the critical mass on your side. These children will often influence the behaviour of the few remaining troublemakers, who start to feel like the odd ones out.

By having a positive approach, you will retain your sense of humour and your sense of perspective. If you can achieve this, you are far less likely to get stressed when things do go wrong. Learn to see everything that happens in your classroom in a positive light, rather than allowing it to make you become cynical and bad tempered.

I do appreciate how easy it can be to slip into a negative approach, particularly if you work in a very difficult school. When things are going badly in the classroom – chairs are being thrown, your students are ignoring you and they simply won't be quiet – it is all too tempting to expect the worst. The tension builds up inside you, even before the class arrives at your lesson. Always remember, though, that not every single student in a class will ever be behaving badly, no matter how much it feels as though they are. Here are some tips for maintaining a positive outlook and teaching style with your children.

- *Focus on what's going well:* When there is lots of misbehaviour in a class, it is easy to focus in on this, and forget about all the things that are going well. Sometimes the best way to deal with a troublemaker is to totally ignore that student, provided the behaviour is not affecting the rest of the class. Praise a student for good work, and show that this is the way to get your attention, rather than allowing poor behaviour to distract you.
- *Focus on your achievements:* Similarly, when faced by poor behaviour on a daily basis, it is easy to lose your sense of perspective. Take a moment to consider all the things that you are achieving with your children. It could be that getting them to stay in their seats, or to listen when you want to address the class, actually represents a huge achievement.
- *Keep yourself fresh:* Teaching can be exhausting, especially at those times of year when there are lots of meetings, parents' evenings and other demands outside of school hours. Although taking part in extra-curricular activities can be an excellent way of developing good teacher–student relationships, do make sure that you don't take on too much. Give yourself some time for a life outside school, and this will help you keep your style fresh and positive.
- *Don't become defensive:* It's hard, but do try not to become defensive when faced by misbehaviour. It is all too easy to slip into a frame of mind where you see everything in the worst possible light. React from your head and not your heart, and don't allow incidents of misbehaviour to cloud your whole style.
- *Use positive language:* By making a simple change in the type of language you use with your students, you can achieve a very positive atmosphere in your classroom. For instance, greet your students by saying, 'Great to see you! I'm really looking forward to the brilliant work you're going to do today!' With such a positive approach, even the most cynical or jaded child will be tempted to live up to your expectations.

6

USING REWARDS
AND SANCTIONS

Why use rewards and sanctions?

Using rewards and sanctions offers us a way of encouraging and enforcing better behaviour. Rewards help us to motivate our students, particularly those who do not have a natural inclination to work hard. Sanctions give us a way of making our students work within the boundaries we have set. If a child does not do 'X' in terms of behaviour, then the result will be sanction 'Y'. The 'carrot and stick' analogy is useful here. We all respond far better to encouragement than to punishment. Bear in mind that responses to both rewards and sanctions will depend on your particular situation – for instance, in some schools detentions are highly effective, in others they are counter-productive.

Some thoughts on rewards

Using rewards is one of the most effective ways of getting better behaviour. Before you even think of applying sanctions, always look first to the rewards that you might use. This will help you maintain a positive focus and atmosphere in your classroom. It's not as simple as indiscriminately handing out hundreds of merits and stickers, though. For rewards to have a direct impact on behaviour, it's important to use them wisely.

We turn up to work at least partly for the tangible reward of receiving a salary – we have a powerful reason to stay motivated. Of course, for many teachers the job is about much more than this. There are many other benefits for us in the work that we do, not least the satisfaction of seeing young people develop and learn. Some students will work hard and behave well without any particular need for extrinsic rewards. These are the children who have been taught the value and importance of school for its own sake. They are able to delay gratification, because they understand the longer-term benefits of getting a good education. Other children will need almost constant rewards and reassurance, because they lack this inner drive and find it very hard to keep themselves motivated.

Some of the best rewards run close to the wind – you will need to decide how far you can or should go in bribing your students. This will depend on your own personal values and also on what your school will allow. For instance, to keep a difficult class focused, you might offer them a highly valued reward of their choice (e.g. listening to music). Although this might not strictly be 'allowed', it could prove very effective as a motivator. It would also win you a reputation as someone who is willing to negotiate.

Here are some general tips about the effective use of rewards. Although much of what follows might seem obvious, it is easy to lose sight of some of these points.

- *Rewards must be wanted:* It's pointless to use rewards that your students don't want. For a reward to have meaning, it must be valued by the students: they must *want* to receive it. Sometimes, teachers are not helped by the rewards their school suggests using in a behaviour policy. These are often out of date or not particularly effective as motivators.
- *Rewards need to be age specific:* Different rewards work best with different age groups. Typically, the older the students, the more they want rewards which have monetary value (CD vouchers, stationery).
- *Rewards must be properly earned:* Make sure that your students earn their rewards fully, rather than handing them out for any old bit of good behaviour or work. The harder they are to get, the more they will be valued. Where rewards are overused by some teachers, this can devalue the currency for the rest of the staff.
- *Fit the reward to the individual:* Within a class, there will be some children who are desperate to get stickers, and others for whom the offer of a phone call home is the ultimate prize. Be specific with your rewards, tailoring them to the individual child as far as possible.
- *Rewards have a sell-by date:* A particular reward might work well at first, then gradually run out of steam as the children get used to receiving it. Regularly refresh the rewards system you use – both as an individual teacher and as a whole school.
- *Reward all your students:* We can get trapped into giving lots of

rewards to our tricky students, to keep them onside and get them to cooperate. But don't overlook those children who work hard all the time – they deserve to receive recognition for their efforts as well.

– *Sometimes rewards need to be private:* Most of the time, rewards can be given publicly. However, in some situations children will not want others to witness their success – the peer group pressure against good work or behaviour is too great. If this is the situation in which you teach, then you might crouch down beside a difficult child who is working well, sharing your positive thoughts in private. Alternatively, you could make a positive comment as you pass a student in the corridor, outside of lesson time.

Types of rewards

My experience suggests that reward systems tend to be very similar from school to school – typically merits, certificates and home/school contacts prevail. There are some schools that are becoming more innovative in the rewards that they offer, and you will find some of these more unusual ideas below. Of course the most valuable reward is free and easy to give – praise from a teacher whom the children respect and like (it's gaining that respect in the first place that's the hard part). Here are some suggestions for more tangible rewards that you might use.

– *Merits/commendations:* In a school where students are reasonably well motivated, commendations or merits can be a good form of reward. Unfortunately, even though this is one of the most commonly used reward systems, it does have its drawbacks. To be perfectly blunt, in many secondary schools merits don't work well past the first year. In addition, the students you most want to motivate may turn their noses up at the idea of getting merits.

– *Points systems:* A useful 'add on' to a merit system is to give the students points for their merits. They can then 'cash in' these points for vouchers, etc.

- *Certificates:* Many schools give their students certificates to reward good behaviour or work, and these are often presented at a whole-school assembly. Certificates can prove effective, and they give the children something tangible to take home.
- *Stickers:* These seem to work well from nursery right up to GCSE level and beyond. You can get personalized stickers that include the teacher's name or the subject. Think about where the students are going to put their stickers – perhaps on a diary or an exercise book.
- *Positive written comments:* Praise written in an exercise book can be very useful in encouraging hard work and good effort. Make sure you set aside time for the students to read your comments when you hand back books.
- *Prizes and awards:* Some schools have a prize day, when students are given awards for work or effort in different areas. With parents in attendance, this can be an excellent motivator.
- *Phoning home:* Although we tend to use phone calls home as a punishment for poor behaviour, they can actually be very effective as a reward. If a student is keen to please his or her parents or guardians, a quick phone call can really have a huge effect on behaviour. Catch one of your difficult students on a good day, promise a phone call home if he or she behaves really well, and start to build a positive relationship. The child's parents will probably be surprised and delighted to hear some positive comments at last. Before phoning, do check first about your school system for home/school contacts.
- *Writing home:* Writing home can be a very powerful reward. A good number of schools are now using postcards, rather than standardized letters. The children could even design the postcards themselves, for instance in an art or design lesson. The great thing about a postcard is that it might be stuck with a magnet on a fridge door, as a constant reminder of the teacher's approval.
- *Trips:* Using the reward of a trip can be a powerful motivator. It has the added benefit of leaving a very positive and beneficial 'afterglow' for those involved. One drawback is that it does require a lot of work to organize this type of event.

- *'Special' time:* Earning privileges can be very effective, and it demonstrates the link between good behaviour and its positive consequences. The idea of a special, or 'golden', time is quite widely used within infant classrooms. The children earn (or lose) the right to an hour at the end of the school week. In this time they are given a free choice of fun activities. Secondary teachers might adapt this idea, for instance offering five minutes' 'golden time' for chat at the end of a lesson.
- *'Special' tasks:* Students love being offered an 'adult' task as a reward, and this can also be useful for the teacher. For instance, tidying the stock cupboard was a real favourite when I was at junior school. Another great one is 'you be teacher', where the child teaches the class for a few minutes. He or she might write up some ideas on the board, give the answers to a test, or even introduce part of a lesson, while you take a well-deserved break.
- *Listening to music:* This is a very popular reward for older students. Whether you use it will depend on your subject: in some lessons background music might distract the students from their work. One word of advice – use the radio, rather than allowing them to bring in music of their own choice, to avoid any problems with inappropriate language.
- *Raffles:* This is one that I've heard a few times recently. The teacher gives out raffle tickets for good work or behaviour, and then holds a draw at the end of the lesson or the week, with a prize given to the winner. Sometimes these raffles are held across the school, and for longer periods of time (e.g. half a term), with really good prizes.
- *Marbles in a jar:* This is a great idea that I was given, and one which utilizes the power of peer pressure. The teacher has an empty jar on his or her desk, and every time a student works hard or behaves well, a marble is put in the jar. When the jar is full, the whole class receives a reward. One suggestion I was given is to hold a class picnic at lunchtime, ordering takeaway pizza for the children.
- *Sweets and other treats:* Obviously it's very much a matter of personal opinion as to whether or not you feel it's appropriate to give out sweets in your classroom. Suffice to say that these do prove a popular motivator with children.

Some thoughts on sanctions

Using sanctions can be a surprisingly complicated business. On the face of it, you should stick closely to the school behaviour policy, or your departmental rules. As far as possible, consistent use of sanctions is best for staff and fairest for students. However, sometimes your school policy will not serve you or your students well, and a little flexibility will be necessary. No one likes to be punished and so, when we are forced to use sanctions, this needs to be done as well as possible. Here are some tips and suggestions for the effective use of sanctions.

- *Sanctions must be unwanted:* In exactly the same way that rewards must be wanted, the sanctions you use must be ones that the students want to avoid. Otherwise, they will not act as an effective deterrent. Again, teachers are often hampered by what is in their school behaviour policy. For instance, if your students don't care about getting detentions, then there is little point in giving them.
- *Sanctions must be followed through:* When you give a sanction, it absolutely *must* be served, otherwise it was pointless giving it in the first place. If the punishment is not served, the next time you threaten it the students will know that this is an empty threat.
- *Don't threaten what you can't or won't deliver:* When we are stressed, it can be tempting to throw out threats about all the terrible things that will happen to the class if they don't stop messing around. Students are very aware of their rights, and about what you can and cannot do to them. A teacher who threatens to keep an entire class behind for an hour that same evening will be laughed out of the room.
- *Avoid the threat of 'somebody else':* Sometimes a teacher will threaten to send a child to 'somebody else' for misbehaviour (typically a senior manager, head of year, house or department, etc.). Unfortunately, all this does is suggest that the teacher cannot deal with the problem by him or herself. When I speak to the 'somebody elses' in a school, they will often complain of lines of students outside their doors during lesson

times. Typically, these students are sent to them by only a limited number of teachers. Of course, there will be some situations where this threat is entirely justified, for instance with incidents of very serious misbehaviour.

- *Sanctions can create a negative atmosphere*: Sanctions can create bad feeling if they are applied too rigidly and without sensitivity about the type of students you teach. In some very difficult schools, it might be better to focus on developing positive relationships with your students, rather than creating confrontation by imposing frequent punishments.

Types of sanctions

There are various types of sanctions that you can use to help you control behaviour in your classroom. As with rewards, schools do tend to be fairly similar in the types of sanctions that they use. How effective these punishments are will of course depend on your situation. Here are some of the options. I've devoted an entirely separate section to detentions below, because using them can be surprisingly complicated.

- *Shouting:* Although not traditionally viewed as a 'sanction', shouting is the most immediate form of punishment you can use with your class, and it is hardly surprising that many teachers resort to it once in a while. Sometimes, having a good shout can be an effective way of letting off steam. Remember, though, that shouting demonstrates a loss of self-control and can be very damaging for your voice.
- *Phoning/writing home:* Never underestimate the power of parents! If you are working with parents who are genuinely supportive, then phoning or writing home can be an extremely effective sanction. If the child understands that poor behaviour will be reported to the home, this offers you a very powerful control mechanism. If, however (as may happen with poorly behaved students), the parents simply do not care, or cannot control the child themselves, then this sanction is not going to be effective. Check on your school

policy before contacting the home, and find out about the home background in case you might be putting the child at risk.

- *Loss of privileges:* Connecting behaviour to the winning or losing of privileges offers a clear way of linking behaviour to its consequences. For instance, if you are using an hour of 'golden time' in your primary classroom, then poor behaviour during the week could lead to the loss of blocks of this time. Those children who have behaved well would retain the whole hour, and get first choice at selecting an activity. Any children who had misbehaved would see a clear link between their behaviour that week and being held back from the privilege.
- *Whole-class sanctions:* In some situations, a whole-class sanction might be appropriate, for instance with a very talkative class. Bear in mind, though, that you will probably be punishing some children who have done nothing wrong at all. When you do use whole-class detentions, let the class 'claw back' the time for good behaviour.
- *The 'ultimate' sanction:* Many schools now have a final sanction whereby a student who is causing excessive disruption, or who is posing a danger to themselves or to others, can be removed from the classroom by a senior teacher. The knowledge that this sanction is available gives the teacher a feeling of safety and reassurance.
- *'Comedy' sanctions:* I've had some fun with these in the past – whether or not you use them will depend on your teaching style and on the likely reaction of the children. I've found that they add a nice touch of humour to my classroom. A comedy sanction might be something like: 'Go and stand in the corner on one leg, with your hands on your head, for one minute.' So long as your students accept these sanctions with good grace, they offer a good way of making a point about misbehaviour while at the same time keeping the tone light and amusing.

Some thoughts on detentions

As one of the most frequently used sanctions, it is vital to get the use of detentions right. Depending on your school situation, detentions may work very well, or they may be of no use at all. You will need to use your professional judgement to decide whether detentions work for you. If they do, then using them effectively can offer you a really valuable tool in managing behaviour.

- *Make sure detentions are served:* Chasing up students can be incredibly time-consuming – that brief moment of poor behaviour in class can turn into a cat-and-mouse game of epic proportions. However, if you are not willing to chase up on missed detentions, you would be better off not using them at all.
- *Get them served as soon as you can:* Ideally, there should be a clear link between the misbehaviour and the punishment, so get detentions served as quickly as possible. It is far better for students to serve that initial short detention, than for you to have to chase them for not turning up, or refer them for more serious sanctions.
- *Use a 'collection service':* In secondary schools, a major problem with getting detentions served is when you need a student to return to you at a break time or at the end of the day. When children fail to turn up, you are then forced into chasing after them to serve the sanction. To avoid this, send a reliable student to go and fetch your detainee a few minutes before the bell goes, agreeing this with their teacher beforehand.
- *Consider what will happen during the detention:* Consider what the children will actually do during detentions. You might take the opportunity to have a chat about why the misbehaviour occurred, and what can be done to stop it happening again. You could devise a community punishment, such as collecting up plates in the dining hall, or picking up rubbish in the classroom. If the sanction is for work not done in class time, then obviously the student will need to finish the work in the detention. Some teachers swear by 'revenge style'

punishments, such as setting lines. Alternatively, you might try the 'bore them into submission' approach and insist that they sit in silence for the entire detention time.

- *Watch how detentions are perceived:* In some schools, or for some children, extra time with the teacher or in the classroom might be viewed as a reward. Where students are nervous about going out into the playground at breaks, detention can seem like an attractive option. Do be aware of how your students perceive time spent in detention, and take this into consideration when using it as a sanction.

How to apply sanctions

When you come to apply sanctions, the way that you do this will have an impact on how the students react. Your application of sanctions will also affect how well the punishments actually work. The idea is to avoid confrontation, giving a series of warnings rising in seriousness, showing that the student is forcing you to actually apply the sanction. Here are some detailed tips about the effective use of sanctions.

- *Keep the sanction private:* Always try to sanction students in a quiet, individual way. You could ask the student to step outside for a moment to talk with you, or take the child to the back of the room. Use a quiet voice, so that the rest of the class can't hear. If the student feels embarrassed to be punished in front of his or her peers, this might lead to a confrontation. Don't give your troublemakers the 'oxygen of publicity'.
- *Defer if necessary:* Don't feel that you always have to give a sanction immediately the misbehaviour occurs. For instance, if you are trying to introduce the lesson and one child is being disruptive, you might say 'I'll come and talk to you about your behaviour in a moment' so that you can complete your introduction. Once the class is on task, you can then deal with the student in relative privacy.
- *Make the situation clear:* Misunderstandings can lead to unnecessary confrontations, so always make your position

crystal clear. State your expectations clearly, telling the student exactly what you want, then clarify how the student's behaviour is failing to meet your expectations.

- *Make your feelings clear:* Explain very clearly to the student how the behaviour is making you feel, and how it is impacting on your lesson, and on the learning of the rest of the class. Encourage your children to see how other people view their behaviour, and consequently why it is unacceptable.
- *Offer a positive alternative to misbehaviour:* Sometimes, students back themselves into a corner when they misbehave, and it is up to the teacher to offer them a way out. For instance, you might use a distraction, giving the child a task to complete, such as handing out resources. The younger the children are, the easier it will be to distract them from misbehaviour.
- *Remember! Repetition is vital:* Repetition will ensure that you are clearly understood. Repeat your warnings several times over, and use the student's name repeatedly to ensure that you have his or her full attention.
- *Tell, don't ask:* Teachers need to assert themselves by the use of positive commands, rather than using questions which give the student the opportunity for a variety of responses. Use *'I want'* and *'I need you to'*, rather than *'Could you'* or *'Will you'*. *Tell* your students exactly what you want them to do – they need to know.
- *Give an explicit warning before further action:* After spelling out the situation in the most definite terms, tell the student what will happen if he or she fails to meet your requirements.
- *Sanction the behaviour, not the student:* See the problem as with the behaviour, and not with the child, and this will help you keep sanctions depersonalized. Make it clear that your use of sanctions is not a personal attack on the student, but a logical and consistent response to the student's behaviour.
- *Use 'the choice':* This strategy, described in Chapter 3, helps you depersonalize sanctions, and throws the responsibility for the situation back on the student. The choice is simple: 'Either you stop the behaviour now, or you will force me to apply this particular sanction.'
- *Stay relaxed during the process:* As you'll see in the 'good'

example below, the teacher's response is very casual and relaxed. Rather than wading in immediately with a sanction, she simply coaxes the child back to her seat by explaining how much fun the lesson is going to be. If you can maintain a cool, easy approach this will help you avoid defensiveness, and assist you in keeping a perspective when you are dealing with difficult students.

- *Apply the sanctions in clear steps:* Your sanctions should start at a low level, and gradually build up if the student continues to defy you. At each stage, give the student the opportunity to accept that level of sanction, before moving on. The teacher who jumps in with the most severe punishment will be viewed as unfair, and this is likely to encourage confrontations.

- *Keep your approach non-confrontational and polite:* Remain relentlessly calm and polite as you apply each level of sanction, however strong the temptation is to blow off steam. Keep a constant check on your use of voice and body language. This gives the student nothing to feed off and a confrontation is less likely to occur.

- *Sound as though you regret the punishment:* Aim to sound rather unhappy and disappointed that the child has forced you to use a sanction. Use a tone of regret rather than one of revenge.

- *Offer a chance to 'back out' or 'claw back':* At each stage of the sanctioning process, give the student a chance to avoid further punishment. If the situation merits, tell the child that if he or she accepts the current sanction with good grace, and works well for the rest of the lesson, it is possible that you may reconsider the punishment.

Here are two examples of a teacher applying a sanction, showing how the student might react to different approaches.

A good way to apply sanctions

Carly has arrived at her science lesson in a very bad mood. She is wandering around the room, chatting to the other students. The teacher is ready to take the register and wants to start the lesson.

Teacher: Carly, I'd like a quick word please.

The teacher motions Carly to come to the back of the classroom. Carly follows.

Teacher: Carly, I want to start my lesson now. And I can't do that with you wandering around the room.

Carly.   So? What are you gonna do about it?

Teacher: Well, Carly, I really want to get on with my lesson. We're going to be mixing some chemicals together to see if they explode. I'm sure you're really going to enjoy it, but you'll need to sit down first so that I can take the register.

Carly: Oh. That sounds quite good.

Teacher: So, come and sit down, and let's get on with it.

Carly returns to her seat and sits down. Later on in the lesson she gets up again and starts to wander around. Again, the teacher motions her to one side.

Teacher: Carly. I told you earlier on to stay in your seat. I want you to sit down now please.

Carly: No I won't. I'm bored. This lesson is stupid.

Teacher: Well, Carly, I'm sorry that you feel that way, but I'm afraid if you continue to behave like this, and refuse to follow my instructions, you will force me to give you a detention.

Carly: That's not fair! I'm not doing anything wrong!

Teacher: Carly. I want you to sit down in your seat and continue with your work. You need to sit down because we're using some dangerous chemicals, and I don't want you to get hurt. Now sit down before I have to give you that detention.

At this stage it is hoped Carly will understand the situation, and will comply with the teacher's request. If she does not, the teacher should apply the sanction, moving up step by step until Carly does what she is told.

A bad way to apply sanctions

Carly has arrived at her science lesson in a very bad mood. She is wandering around the room, chatting to the other students. The teacher is ready to take the register and wants to start the lesson.

Teacher: Carly! Can you sit down please? I want to start my lesson.

Carly: Well, I don't want to start your lesson. Your lessons are stupid.

Teacher: Don't be so rude! Look, why can't you just sit down and let me get on with taking the register?

The rest of the class are watching the confrontation with interest. Carly is now enjoying the 'publicity' of being sanctioned in front of the class.

Carly: No, I won't sit down. Are you gonna make me?

Teacher: Yes I am going to make you. You're in an hour's detention with me after the lesson.

Carly: That's not fair! I'm not coming to your stupid detention!

Teacher: Yes you are. Now shut up and sit down.

The class are getting restless. Some of them are starting to chat and giggle about what is going on.

Carly: You can't tell me to shut up! I hate you and I hate your lessons. I'm out of here!

Carly storms out of the room. The rest of the class are now totally distracted and it takes the teacher another ten minutes to settle them down.

7

TEACHING FOR
GOOD BEHAVIOUR

Teaching and behaviour

It's important to keep in mind that the reason we need to manage behaviour at all is so that we can actually get on with teaching. That's what we're in the classroom for, after all. Those teachers who are able to plan and deliver really high-quality lessons will, a fair amount of the time, get well-behaved students. Of course there will be some situations where the children make it impossible for you to get as far as actually doing any teaching. However, if you make your lessons well structured, interesting, fast paced and engaging, this will help you keep the students in line most of the time. After all, if the children spend the majority of the lesson time really engaged with their work, they are far less likely to think about messing around.

Of course, not every lesson can be an all-singing, all-dancing, multimedia extravaganza. There will be days when you are so tired that you can barely drag yourself into school; other times when the subject being taught is dry and dull and hard to spice up. But if most of your lessons are high-quality ones, then your children will inevitably be more inclined to behave themselves for you. A teacher who offers the students engaging lessons will gain a good reputation within the class or across the school. Your students will be discussing you outside of class time. If the feeling is that your lessons are fun and interesting, they will turn up at your classroom in a positive mood, expecting the best.

There is, of course, a balance to be struck between what students view as fun activities and what is educational. After all, given the choice, many children would spend all day every day playing computer games, or out on the football pitch. You, of course, are required to teach them the curriculum. Inevitably, it will be difficult to make some of the material you must teach stimulating, while still covering all subject areas. On the whole, though, children will forgive the occasional dull lesson from a teacher who normally teaches in an inspirational way.

If you think back to your own schooldays, I hope that you too can remember one or more teachers who really inspired you, who filled you with a passion for learning or for a particular subject. Who perhaps even inspired you to become a teacher yourself. Being in a position to inspire the next generation is an incredible honour for us as teachers. Although teaching with passion, energy and enthusiasm can be hard work at times, it is well worth it in terms of the potential benefits for your children.

Effective planning and teaching

There is great skill involved in planning and delivering high-quality lessons. Learning how to plan and teach well takes time, but eventually you get a feel for what is going to be effective. With experience you also learn how to adapt your teaching for different classes and different children – sometimes even during the lesson itself. Planning quality lessons should be relaxing and enjoyable for the teacher. It requires you to use your imagination, and to think laterally about different ways of putting across a subject.

As a student teacher, lesson planning is expected to include lots of detail (to my mind, often too much detail). If you are currently studying to be a teacher, you will need to play the game and plan as your lecturers expect you to plan. In any case, a detailed plan will help you think through your lessons in advance and also give you a sense of security.

However, once you qualify and begin to experiment, you might find (as I do) that too much prescriptive planning tends to work against good-quality lessons. Having too much detail in your plan might tempt you to stick to something that obviously isn't working. It might also 'stick you' to your desk so that you can keep an eye on your notes, while misbehaviour is rife at the back of the room. Detailed planning in advance suggests that the teacher knows exactly how the children are going to respond. However, what has worked well in the past with one class might fail hopelessly with another. With experience you will learn how to adapt your lessons as they actually take place.

The ability to engage, interest and excite your students will depend on a whole range of different factors – the format and content of a lesson, and also the way it is delivered. The suggestions given below will help you plan and teach the type of lessons that are most likely to get you good behaviour in return.

The format of lessons

Lesson format is the 'nuts and bolts' of good planning – it's about giving a clear and effective structure to class time. Generally speaking, children love to have structure in their lives, and this structure is often particularly important for those students with behaviour issues. Good lesson format and design will help you keep your students focused and on task. Use the suggestions below to help you format your lessons effectively.

- *Give them a 'map':* When you have spent time preparing a lesson, it is tempting to believe that the students will somehow 'know' what it is going to be about, without any explanation. When the teacher simply launches straight into the subject, the children feel a lack of clear structure or purpose, and are more likely to start messing around. This is where ideas such as aims, objectives, learning intentions, learning outcomes, etc. come in. It doesn't really matter what you call this, so long as you give your students a 'map' at the beginning of the lesson. This 'map' tells them what is going to happen ('we are going to learn this today') and why ('we need to learn this because'). As the lesson proceeds, refer back to this lesson purpose frequently to keep the students (and yourself) on track. Many teachers now write their learning objectives on the board to act as a visual prompt. Sometimes, a lesson will deviate entirely from the original purpose or intention. This isn't necessarily a problem, so long as it is a result of teachers adapting to suit the students, rather than simply losing their way.
- *Keep the tasks short and focused:* The longer you spend on any one activity, the more chance there is for the students to get bored. With lots of short, purposeful exercises, you can create a strong sense of focus and set clear targets for your students to achieve. You can then reward the completion of each target before you move on to the next. Using short, focused tasks

creates a sense of pace and forward momentum which is useful in engaging those students with poor attention spans.

- *Keep the lessons varied:* Use a mix and match approach – ensure that there is plenty of variety in the types of tasks you do. This will help you appeal to different learning styles – something aural, something visual, something active. When you do have to teach a section of the curriculum that is teacher-led, follow it with a chance for some group or project work. Use a variety of exercises within each lesson, from class brainstorms to paired discussions, from drawing and artwork to writing or note taking.

- *Give details of what you want your students to achieve:* Create a sense of purpose by telling the students exactly how much they need to achieve during each task, whether this is ten words, three ideas, or half a page. A useful tip I was once given is to split longer tasks up into work you *must* do, work you *should* do, and work you *could* do. These three categories give the students a clear target at which to aim. The more able will probably finish all three parts of the work. The less able students know that there is a certain amount that must be completed if they are to avoid a sanction.

- *Give details of what your students have achieved:* At the end of your lessons, talk with your students about what they have achieved, and take the time to reward them for their hard work. Create a positive sense of success, so that they are more likely to behave and work well the next time you see them. This review time (or what is now often referred to as a 'plenary') gives a good sense of completion to a lesson.

The content of lessons

Planning and delivering the content of a lesson is (or should be) where the fun lies. Our role as teachers is in putting ideas, facts or information across so that the children understand them. Making a subject accessible to all students can provide you with a great sense of achievement, as well as helping keep your children on task and behaving themselves. The ideas given below will help you in planning and delivering high-quality content in your lessons.

- *Make it fun:* Making work seem like 'fun' often involves a bit of lateral thinking. Students tend to view lessons as fun if they seem as little like work as possible, or if they are connected to something from 'real life' outside of school. This is part of the reason why my crime scene lesson (see below) is so effective. A quiz, as opposed to a test, is an easy and entertaining way to check your students' understanding of a topic. Keep an eye out for fun and educational games that you can use, perhaps alternating them with more conventional work as a reward for good effort.

- *Make it sensory:* We normally ask our children to use only a limited palette of senses in a lesson – typically their sight and their hearing. Find ways to incorporate activities that involve the three other senses. Get them touching objects, smelling different plants, or tasting a range of foods.

- *Use lots of props and resources:* Children love getting their hands on *things* during lesson time, particularly things that are not normally found in the classroom. Look at the section below ('Using resources') for lots of ideas.

- *Make it topical and relevant:* Match the work to your students' interests, or to current events in the news or media. This will help them stay motivated, make them take the learning more seriously, and show them that school does actually relate to the wider world beyond. For instance, you might use a link to a sports event such as the football World Cup to introduce some geography work on different flags.

- *Make it big, colourful and eye-catching:* All these approaches will appeal to your children, particularly those who enjoy more visual ways of learning. Think big – take the class outside to draw an enormous brainstorm on the playground floor. Use vivid colours to get their attention, or eye-catching displays to make them think.

- *Turn abstract concepts into concrete activities:* One of the skills of the teacher is to find ways to put across tricky, abstract ideas in a way that children can understand. Where you have to teach an abstract concept (division, metaphor, gravity), find ways to make it concrete. To give an example, I once watched a science lesson where the teacher used a skateboard to demonstrate forces, and to show how a rocket can escape the earth's gravitational pull. A student stood on the skateboard and swung his arms from side to side, making it move slightly. He then pushed off from another student, making it move even further. He finished by swinging and then throwing a weight, propelling the skateboard across the room.

The delivery of lessons

Effective lesson delivery is as much about teacher style and personality as it is about good-quality planning. The suggestions given earlier about verbal and non-verbal communication and teaching styles (see Chapters 4 and 5) will all help you deliver your lessons in the best possible way. On the whole, teachers who can communicate a sense of passion for the subject, of love for the process of learning, and of interest in their students, will tend to naturally inspire good behaviour in their children.

The importance of time management

The way that a teacher controls time in the classroom can have a surprisingly positive or negative effect on behaviour. If your lessons feel rushed, your students will feel stressed and are more likely to misbehave. Aim to achieve a calm, measured approach, with each task having a suitable quantity of time allocated to it. Teachers will often plan to do far too much during a lesson, and consequently find themselves rushing to fit everything in. Try to be flexible about what you can achieve within the lesson time. If your students are poorly behaved, it is likely that you will have to spend some of the lesson sanctioning them, leaving you less time to complete the work.

The beginning and end of each lesson are times when you can feel the need to rush to get started or finished. However, when aiming for control of behaviour, these are times of crucial importance. Spend whatever time is necessary bringing your class into your room and settling them down. Some classes respond well to a 'quick start', where the teacher plunges straight into the lesson; others need time to settle and get themselves in the right mood for work. Again, plan your lessons so that you leave enough time at the end to finish calmly, perhaps factoring in an opportunity to reflect on what has been achieved during the lesson. Here are some specific ideas for managing time more effectively in your lessons.

- *Use a whole-class focus:* At the start of each lesson, spend some time pulling the whole class together. This is especially important after a break, when the children need to regain their focus on work. It is also helpful in the secondary school, where the students are moving between different subject areas. A whole-class focus might be as simple as asking the children to close their eyes while you take the register. It could be a more specific activity, such as everyone counting out loud from twenty to zero simultaneously, or playing some name games.
- *Take regular breaks:* Using a series of short tasks gives a lesson a good sense of pace and momentum. Taking breaks between each task offers an opportunity for the children to refresh themselves. Your break might consist of a short time to discuss the work with a partner. You might set a physical or mental activity for the whole class to break up the stretches of hard work. For instance, the old favourite of rubbing one hand in circles on the stomach, whilst patting the other hand on the head.
- *Always aim to finish early:* In my own classroom experience, having to rush a lesson as it draws to a close, or having to carry on after the bell goes, is guaranteed to cause stress and tension for the students and the teacher. I would always recommend aiming to finish early and with a sense of calm, even if this means that you have some time left over to use up at the end of the lesson.
- *Pull the class together for a review:* At the end of each lesson, a good way to create a positive sense of achievement is to pull the class together in a review, now often referred to as a 'plenary', of what has been attained during the lesson. Looking back over what has been learned will help con-

solidate the work in your students' minds. It also offers a useful opportunity to reward your children for their hard work and good behaviour.

- *Send them away in the right frame of mind:* When they next see you, whether this is the following day in a primary school, or the next week in a secondary school, you want your children to have a positive memory of your last experience together. The final minutes of your previous lesson together will be freshest in their minds, and if they remember these as a calm and well-ordered time, this is likely to create a climate for better behaviour. One useful activity for finishing the lesson in the right frame of mind is to use a 'statues' exercise. The children freeze completely still for a couple of minutes (either sitting or lying down). On your signal they then push their chairs behind the desks, as quietly as possible. This can be done in slow motion to create more interest.

Guaranteed to succeed

Some days you will not be in the mood to cope with the difficult classes that you might have to teach, and it is on these occasions that you need some lessons pretty much guaranteed to encourage good behaviour. There really is no need to feel guilty for wanting the occasional lesson off from coping with misbehaviour. We are only human, and no one can work at full steam all the time. Teaching is, in many ways, like acting, in that we are presenting ourselves to a large (and often difficult) audience. Nobody could realistically expect an actor to perform all day every day, and the same applies to the exhausted teacher. The suggestions below are for lessons practically guaranteed to succeed even with the most difficult students/classes. They have worked for me in a variety of schools, from the 'fairly easy' to the 'downright impossible'!

- *The computer room:* For some reason, putting a student in front of a computer will encourage even the most poorly behaved to work well (or at least to keep still and quiet while they log on

103

to the Internet). Most curriculum areas offer at least some opportunities for using computers, so take advantage of this fact when you need a peaceful hour.

- *Show a video:* Even the most terribly behaved classes will usually sit fairly quietly to watch a video. Assuage your guilt by ensuring this is related to a subject they are currently studying. Frame it as a 'treat' that the class have earned because of recent good behaviour. Make sure the video is relatively up to date, and interesting enough to keep your students' attention. Before the lesson, ensure that the equipment is working, otherwise you might face chaos as you try to set it up. To focus the class's attention, you might set some written tasks or some questions for the children to answer after watching the video.

- *Use an 'engaging lesson':* A lesson that will engage your students usually offers them something different, something unusual, something adult, or something with 'props', such as the 'crime scene' described below. Although these lessons take quite a lot of planning, they will certainly make your life easier during the actual class time. They will also help you gain that vital reputation for being an interesting or exciting teacher.

- *Bring in an outside helper:* In my experience, students respond really well to people who are not teachers. Perhaps they are too used to seeing us every day, to hearing our voices and suffering the punishments we give them. If you can organize someone to come in from outside, a theatre group to perform a play, a police officer to talk about drugs, or a parent to discuss careers, you'll earn yourself a nice easy 'lesson off'.

'Engaging' lessons across the curriculum

This section gives you a few ideas that I have used, or seen used, to engage a difficult (or even an easy) class. Some of these suggestions might seem a bit bizarre, but remember, if your students are not well motivated in school, the craziest ideas could help to engage them. And in addition to this, you can have some good fun as well. For each idea, I give some of the curriculum areas to which the lesson might relate, the requirements for teaching it, and a description of what actually happens. Thanks very much to the teachers who shared these wonderful ideas with me in the first place. If you're interested in these kinds of engaging lessons, there are lots more ideas in my book *Letting the Buggers be Creative* (Continuum, 2005).

The scene of the crime

Possible curriculum areas:
- History (examining evidence)
- English (literature, e.g. *Romeo and Juliet*)
- Drama (the crime genre)
- Design technology (drawing a plan)
- Science (testing samples, forensic evidence)

Requirements:
- An open space (could be the middle of a classroom with the chairs pushed aside).
- 'Police tape' (you can buy this at www.uktapes.com) or some other barrier around the crime scene.
- Various props that relate to the crime which has been committed. (For example, a chair that has been knocked over, a handbag with the contents spilt out, a bottle and a length of rope.)

Description:
Originally used for a drama lesson, this one grabs the attention of the most rowdy class. You should find that your students quite readily go along with the 'fiction' of the lesson. When they enter the room, the students are told that there has been a crime. They must not touch anything (they will want to) – ask them why and they'll tell you all about fingerprints.

The class work as police detectives to examine the crime scene, discussing their findings and then, depending on the subject, drawing/writing or otherwise responding to the stimulus.

The can of dog food

Possible curriculum areas:
- Design technology (packaging)
- Art (designing a label)
- Media (the power of persuasion)
- Science (analysing the contents of the tin)

Requirements:
- An empty can of dog (or cat) food (preferably well washed).
- Mars bars (chopped up).
- Jelly.
- A fork.

Description:
Originally used for a design technology lesson, this one shocks the students into paying attention. Once the class is in the room, the teacher shows the students the can of dog food, and then proceeds to eat from it. You may find quite a lively reaction to this, but your students should soon quieten down to hear what you have to say about the disgusting taste.

The class can then examine how we believe what we see on packaging, or test the contents of various cans to see what they contain. (The dog food actually is mashed up Mars bars and jelly, by the way.)

The market

Possible curriculum areas:
- Modern foreign languages (vocabulary)
- Maths (money, prices, adding and subtracting)
- Art/design technology (planning and mapping)
- Drama (character work, improvisation)

Requirements:
- 'Market stalls' (could be classroom tables).
- Food or other goods for the stalls.
- 'Money'.

Description:
This lesson was originally used for a French lesson, where the stalls sold different types of French food, and the students had to go around and buy them using the correct vocabulary. The students responded extremely well to the idea of buying tasty croissants and then getting to eat them.

The lesson could be adapted so that the stalls sell any type of object that relates to the subject, or to the resources which you have available. After visiting the market, the class might draw a plan of where the stalls were, or the entire lesson could be a drama improvisation with the students acting out various scenes at the market.

Using resources

Students do respond very well to resources in general, and especially those that are out of the ordinary. The more resources you can bring into your classroom to use, the more you will find the behaviour of your students improving, and the strength of your reputation developing. Resources come in many different shapes and sizes, and it is often unexpected resources that have the most positive results. Remember that resources are not just objects that you bring into the classroom; they can also be other people. Children tend to react well to a person who is not their usual teacher. Why not ask another teacher to come into your classroom to impart some specialist knowledge, or some students from higher up the school to come and work with your children on their reading? Here are some ideas about unusual and engaging resources for you to try.

-   *The magic box:* The teacher brings a box into the classroom, and tells the children that it is a magic box, which can only be opened by using the right spell. The children talk about what might be inside the box, whether they should risk opening it, and what the spell could be that unlocks the box. This resource could lead on to a variety of different writing or drawing activities.

- *The video camera:* If you have access to a video or digital camera, it really can provide a wonderful resource for engaging and motivating your students. The responsibility of using the camera can also be given as a reward for good behaviour over a number of lessons, as the students plan and prepare for actually making a film. The video that you make might be related to a whole range of different subjects. For instance, a 'Safety First' video in a PE class, or a 'Ban the Bullies' video for PSHE.
- *Costumes and wigs:* Although traditionally the province of drama teachers, costumes and wigs can in fact be used to great effect in engaging students in a whole range of subject areas. You might use costumes to introduce vocabulary in a modern foreign languages lesson. You could dress up yourself as a mad professor to do a science experiment. Anything to captivate your children and engage their attention.
- *Sound and lighting:* Schools can be rather dull, unimaginative places, and one way to encourage good behaviour is to add a little atmosphere to your classroom. You might use a sound effects tape of a storm while doing work about the weather; you could black out the room and use torches to read ghost stories; you might play some gentle background music to calm an unruly class. The more unusual and special you can make your classroom appear to the children, the more they will be engaged with the work that they do.

Part Three

THE STUDENTS

8

WHY DO
STUDENTS
MISBEHAVE?

The reasons for student misbehaviour

Of course, there are a whole range of complex reasons behind student misbehaviour. Where a child has serious problems in behaving, there will normally be a range of contributory factors at work. In this chapter, I deal with those areas over which the teacher can have some direct control, or where you have a reasonable chance of making an impact by using specific strategies or approaches.

When you face misbehaviour all or most of the time, it can be tempting to feel that this misbehaviour is premeditated. When a well-planned and well-managed lesson goes wrong, it is natural to become defensive. You put a great deal of hard work into your lessons: why don't your students appreciate this? Surely, you start to believe, they have ganged together beforehand and decided to disrupt your lessons? And the belief that they're 'out to get you' can quickly develop into a defensive teaching style. While it is certainly true that there are some students who make a conscious decision to misbehave, in reality the majority of poor behaviour stems from very different factors. You will find ideas below for solving some of the most common issues.

Of course, in some schools it is the overall ethos at fault, or an ineffective senior management team, or a useless behaviour policy. In other schools, it is about the sheer weight of numbers of children from difficult backgrounds, or with serious special needs. Unfortunately, the individual classroom teacher can have little real impact in these situations, beyond doing his or her best for the students. It is very much a personal decision about how much stress you are willing to take, and the likelihood of an improvement in the near future. If you do find yourself working in a particularly challenging situation, the last chapter of this book gives some advice on handling stress.

School and learning

Boredom

School simply doesn't suit some people. If you think back to your own schooldays, you can probably remember times when you were bored out of your mind. If a student has been taught that school is important, and learning a vital tool for future life, they will put up (on most occasions) with this feeling of boredom, without resorting to misbehaviour. However, if children have learned to see school as a trap, as a place where they are forced to stay despite their lack of interest, it is likely that they will misbehave when they are bored, either to dissipate the feelings of boredom, or to add some interest to lesson time. Winding up the teacher or getting the class to mess around will inevitably seem more interesting to the children than studying some dry and dull topics.

Dealing with boredom

The obvious answer to dealing with boredom would seem to be: make school more interesting! If I think back to my teaching practices at college, I can remember having plenty of time to plan exciting and interesting lessons to engage my students. However, things are not quite so easy for practising teachers, who have so many other demands on their time. In addition, there are the pressures of 'getting through the curriculum' and 'applying the national strategies'. This can mean that you are sometimes forced into delivering boring lessons or creating a timetable that focuses too much on certain subject areas.

It therefore becomes a question of priorities – if you know for a fact that your students have a low level of concentration, and succumb easily to the temptation to misbehave, then you will need to make 'dealing with boredom' one of your main concerns. Put curriculum concerns to one side for a while, and re-engage them with the process of learning. Here are a few suggestions about how you might do this.

- *Make the work fun and interesting:* If you can get your students viewing the lessons as fun, rather than as work, they are less likely to become bored, restless and disruptive.
- *Make the work seem real and meaningful:* Some students don't feel that school relates to their everyday lives. Show how the work you do in lessons has links to jobs that your students might do in later life, or to topics that interest them.
- *Use lots of variety in your lessons:* Students with a low boredom threshold find it hard to focus on one activity for any length of time. Keep your lessons varied, use lots of different exercises and plenty of practical and active work.
- *Use all the senses:* Spice up the work by using sensory activities. Try using some blindfolds to block out sight while focusing on smell, touch, taste or hearing.
- *Keep the tasks short and focused:* For students with short attention spans, use lots of short tasks rather than one or two longer ones. Give praise when each task is finished, or a reward of some type to encourage further effort.
- *Offer a 'get-out' clause:* Sometimes, a restless student or class will need a 'get-out' clause, for instance five minutes off from work for a chat. Know when applying a bit of flexibility is better than flogging a dead horse.
- *Do a deal:* A class that gets interesting and exciting lessons most of the time will generally be willing to put up with the occasional period of boredom. Where you do have to teach a dry subject, ask them to bear with you in return for some fun stuff in the future. Similarly, you might do a deal whereby a class works really hard for twenty minutes, then gets a five-minute break to chat and relax.

Lack of motivation to learn

There is a difference between a student who is bored by school, and a student who lacks the motivation to work. Some students lose their motivation because they find the work too hard, perhaps because they have a specific learning difficulty. Other students might have a fear of failure, or some kind of mental block about a particular subject. If we can match the work closely to each student's abilities, then we will perhaps be able to remotivate them. Other students lack motivation to learn simply because they have never been taught that learning is important, or that it can be fun.

Dealing with lack of motivation to learn

There are many ideas in this book about how you can make your lessons fun, interesting and engaging, particularly in Chapter 7. And if you can achieve this, you might be able to turn your students back on to the whole idea of school, and of learning – a wonderful achievement for any teacher! Here are a few more ideas about how to deal with a demotivated student or class:

- Make the learning that will take place in the lesson very clear, by stating your aims at the start of the lesson.
- Make the reasons for the learning very obvious, perhaps by connecting what happens in class to a job that the student might do after school.
- Divide the lesson into individual tasks and set targets for exactly how much the student must complete in each section.
- Offer rewards for completing each part of a learning task, to encourage the students to see education as rewarding.
- Encourage the children to find 'learning partners' – other students they can work with who will motivate and encourage them, keeping them on task.
- Find out where the demotivated child's talents lie (for instance in drawing or on the computer), and include some of these activities in your lessons, to develop a sense of success.
- Sometimes the problem is because the work is too easy, rather than too hard. Introduce some areas that will really stretch the class or the student – children often respond really well to work that they feel is beyond their age range. Make it clear that you are trusting them to take this difficult, 'adult' work seriously.

Lack of interest in the subjects

It is a fact of life that some students are simply not all that interested in some of the subjects that they are taught. Perhaps the subjects don't seem relevant to them and their experience of the world, or perhaps they have a lack of aptitude for certain areas of the curriculum. The current trend for specialist schools obviously aims to capitalize on students with talents in a particular subject area. Some subjects have, unfortunately, developed a rather negative image. I know from talking with teachers of modern foreign languages that subject perception can cause difficulties in managing behaviour.

In the primary school, the teacher might notice a worsening of behaviour in literacy lessons, or in art sessions. Because the class teacher sees the child in all the subject areas, it can be slightly easier to find ways of getting around an apparent lack of interest or ability in one specific lesson. In the secondary school, a student who behaves impeccably in PE or drama might be a nightmare to teach in English, and vice versa. The English teacher might come to view this student as really difficult, and be surprised to hear that he or she succeeds in more practical subject areas.

Dealing with lack of interest in the subjects

Again, the obvious answer to this problem is to get your students more interested in those subjects they view in a negative way. If you are a secondary teacher working within your subject specialism, your own subject will of course be your passion – your favourite curriculum area. You need to find ways to show the students how interesting and exciting this subject can be. Here are some suggestions about doing this.

- Find out what really interests your class, and use these areas of the curriculum to deliver your subject. For example, if you teach French, and your students are fascinated by computers, spend some lesson time creating menus, or postcards, or a vocabulary book, on the computer. If you teach history, and

114

your students are keen on drama, then use lots of role-play and speaking and listening activities.

- At secondary level, get an overview of any difficult individuals across the different curriculum areas. Talk to other staff (or to the student) to see where the child's strengths and interests lie, and incorporate some aspects of these into your own lessons.
- Check that apparent lack of interest is not a symptom of an unidentified special need. Some children with literacy problems will disguise their difficulty by pretending not to be interested in the lessons.
- At primary level, where a whole class has issues with a particular subject, then use the lure of other more exciting lessons to keep them on task. If they want the reward of the fun stuff, they must work hard in all their subjects.
- Set up some whole-school, departmental or cross-curricular projects to up the level of interest in particularly unpopular subjects. For instance, if maths has a tricky reputation in your school, then hold a 'fun with maths' day to show how exciting it can be.
- Make very clear links between the subject and real-life jobs and people. For example, if you are teaching Spanish and a famous footballer moves to Spain, get the class to prepare a welcome pack for him.

The students

Special needs

Special needs can of course be an important factor in misbehaviour, and not just for those students with a specific emotional or behavioural difficulty. Where a child is struggling with the work, and the teacher does not manage to make it accessible, it is almost inevitable that there will be problematic behaviour. Before you meet your students for the first time, find out who has special needs and how their needs will impact on you as their class teacher. If a student does have a specific learning difficulty, for instance with literacy, it is your responsibility to know about that problem and take it into account. This will have an impact not just in English lessons, but right across the curriculum. It is all too easy to interpret learning difficulties incorrectly, leading to misbehaviour which could be avoided by a full understanding. There is more detailed information on dealing with special needs in the next chapter.

Peer pressure

When we find ourselves in a large group of people, our natural inclination is to 'follow the herd', and behave in a way in which we might not behave if we were on our own. Peer pressure can be a crucial factor in student misbehaviour, particularly in those classes where the number of tricky children is quite high. There is a great deal of pressure on young people to follow their friends, to win the approval of those who work alongside them. By misbehaving, students can achieve a great deal of positive reinforcement from their peers. If they manage to make the whole class laugh at the teacher, this gives them a great deal of status within the group. There is also a fear that if they don't 'follow the crowd', they will appear to be an outsider and will consequently be open to abuse, such as bullying. It is extremely difficult for anyone, let alone young people, to have the courage to stand out from the crowd. If the majority of the class are involved in misbehaviour, it takes a very strong will not to simply go along with them.

Dealing with peer pressure

It can be extremely difficult if the bulk of your class is misbehaving. Dealing with one or two incidents of misbehaviour within a generally well-mannered group is fairly straightforward – you simply take the troublemakers aside and 'sort them out'. However, if the whole class is talking, or refusing to cooperate with you, panic can quickly set in, and you might find yourself shouting, becoming defensive, and generally getting completely stressed out. Here are a few ideas for dealing with the problems caused by peer pressure.

116

- *Impose a whole-class sanction:* Show your students that peer pressure to behave in a certain way is not acceptable. You are in charge, and you have a definite idea about how your class will behave. In a situation where the whole class is talking, and refusing to listen to you, try writing your punishment on the board. Eventually a more observant member of the class will see what you have written and 'shush' the others.
- *Focus on the positive:* Even where it feels like the entire class is misbehaving, it is likely that there will be a handful of children who are doing as you wish. Focus your energy and attention on these students, praising and rewarding them for their good behaviour. If there is a culture of bullying in your school, do be a little bit careful about singling out individuals in front of the class. Take well-behaved students aside after the lesson to thank them for their contributions.
- *Rearrange the seating:* In many situations there will be enough well-behaved children to enable you to separate the tricky ones out. Put any potential troublemakers next to those least likely to fall under their influence. Although it might seem rather unfair to these hard-working students, if it helps you get on with teaching, they are going to prefer it to the alternative of being unable to learn at all.
- *Get the 'ringleader' on your side:* In most group situations, one or two individuals are in charge. It will usually be fairly obvious who the ringleader is in your class. Make a particular effort to get that student on your side, and you will find that the rest of the class quickly follows the lead. While I am not suggesting that you pander to an individual student, establish what motivates his or her misbehaviour, and find ways of dealing with it.
- *Offer an alternative model:* Eventually, if you follow the advice given in this book, your students will understand that there is an alternative. In the end 'teacher pressure' will win out over 'peer pressure', so do persevere.

Lack of self-discipline

As we grow older, we learn that we must have self-discipline if we are to succeed in life. We might not want to get up at

7 o'clock every morning to go to work, but we know that if we want the reward of a salary we have to grit our teeth and get on with it. Some of our students have not yet learned the skills of self-control, self-discipline and concentration. This might be because they come from a home background where these skills are not taught, valued or modelled.

It can be hard for students with little self-discipline to cope with school. For instance, when faced with a huge open gym or playing field in a PE lesson, they might never have had so much space to contend with. It is hardly surprising then that they might run around and test out the new boundaries that are facing them.

Dealing with lack of self-discipline

We need to train our students in the art of self-discipline, if we are going to get them to behave as we wish. Self-discipline and concentration go hand in hand, and all teachers know how important concentration is for effective learning. As a drama teacher, concentration is one of a number of basic skills that I teach my students. Here are a few of the exercises that I use, ones that you could adapt to your own age range or subject speciality. These focus exercises can help settle a lively class at the start of a lesson. Alternatively, you might like to end your lesson or school day with some of these activities, preparing your students to leave in a calm state of mind. Focus exercises are essentially a form of meditation, where we focus on one thing for a length of time, blocking out the myriad distractions of the school environment.

- *Listening:* Ask your students to close their eyes and listen very carefully to the sounds around them, inside the classroom and beyond it into the corridors. They should listen for a minute or two. When the time finishes and they open their eyes, ask them about what they heard.
- *Counting:* Ask the children to shut their eyes and count backwards from fifty to zero. When they get to zero they should open their eyes and wait for the lesson to begin.

- *Backwards spelling:* Ask your children to shut their eyes and spell some words backwards in their heads. For instance, their full names or some key terms from the lesson.
- *Statues:* Get the students into a comfortable position and then freeze them completely still for a length of time (start with a minute or two, then work upwards). You can make the exercise into a test, challenging your class to improve each time. It is amazing how readily students of all ages will do this activity.

The teacher

Although it is of course entirely unintentional, some teachers (perhaps all teachers) do contribute personally to their students' misbehaviour. If you think back to your own schooldays, you will know that there were some teachers for whom all or most of the students misbehaved. Have a think about why this was and whether you too make some of the same mistakes that your own teachers made.

By following the tips in this book, you will be able to stop yourself from encouraging misbehaviour most of the time. Here is a checklist of 'cardinal sins' that you should avoid at all costs. Ask yourself – which of these mistakes do I tend to make? If you bear that particular weak spot in mind, you may be able to catch yourself in the act and prevent trouble in the future.

The 'cardinal sins'

- *Winding them up:* Do you engage your classes in lots of frenzied activities in an attempt to keep them occupied? Do most lessons seem to end up in chaos, and with you feeling completely frazzled? Remember – staying calm is the key, and this includes keeping your students calm too.
- *Being vague or uncertain:* Do you sometimes feel that your children are more in charge of the situation than you are? Where the teacher appears to hand over control to the class, and is uncertain about what he or she actually wants, the students are honour bound to push at the boundaries.

119

- *Being rude:* Do you talk to your students rudely? Do you use phrases like 'shut up' and 'don't be stupid'? Your students are people too – talk to them as you would to an adult, no matter how much they provoke you.
- *Overreacting:* Do you get wound up very easily, reacting to minor misbehaviour as though it were an affront against civilization? Don't forget that your children are just that – children! It is normal and natural for there to be at least some low-level messing around in your classroom.
- *Being confrontational:* Do you 'take on' your students when they misbehave, battling against them in a tit-for-tat competition of wills? I know how tempting it is to respond aggressively, but this can encourage confrontations that might end in physical violence.
- *Being bad-tempered:* Imagine sitting in a classroom faced by a teacher who is constantly in a bad mood. Day after day he or she appears and nags at you, moans at you, complains about the smallest things. And you are forced to sit there and take it. I think that I'd misbehave in this situation – wouldn't you?
- *Being negative:* Are your first words on meeting your class, 'I hope you're not going to behave as badly as last time'? If they are, you may be committing the cardinal sin of negativity. Remember – frame everything you say in a positive light.
- *Being boring:* Have you lost your spark – the bit of you that made you come alive as a teacher? Be honest, are your lessons a bit dull with lots of emphasis on completing worksheets? If they are, then the children may well be messing around to stop themselves from falling asleep.

How students change

Students in the first year at any school are just finding their way around, getting to know the layout of the buildings, and the way that primary, middle, or secondary school actually works. This lack of knowledge about school systems means that they are far more malleable, and you can mould them to your way of thinking, behaving and working. By the time they reach the last year of the school, however, the students have reached the top of the heap. Their increased status means that they will probably start to test the boundaries, and incidents of misbehaviour are more likely to occur.

The following descriptions of students at different ages in their schooling are brief, general guides to some of the factors which may affect their behaviour. Perhaps we sometimes forget what it was like to be young – to be facing a new school for the first time, or the confusion that changes in our bodies and our emotions brought us when we were adolescents. Thinking back to these times in your past will help you offer a greater degree of empathy to your students.

The primary school student

When they first start at school, children are little tiny people. They may be completely overwhelmed by the setting and all the different things that they have to find out. This is often their first lengthy encounter with adults other than their parents or carers, and school can be a confusing and scary place for them. Little wonder, then, that they might be naughty. In an attempt to test what is acceptable behaviour in this strange, new situation, children may 'act out' in undesirable ways. These very young children are entering an environment where many new things are expected of them. Some children may not have previously experienced the behaviours that the teacher requires, such as sitting still on the carpet or concentrating on an activity for an extended period of time.

In addition to finding the new setting strange and confusing, children of this age have little idea of what others think and feel, a very limited ability to empathize. It is only as they grow older that children realize that their bad behaviour may make others (children or adults) feel unhappy and upset. When I did my first teaching practice at a primary school, I was amazed by how little children of this age actually knew. I tried to teach a geography lesson using a globe, but my reception-aged class proved to be completely unaware of the greater world around them. All their encounters up to this stage had been on a very local scale, a fact that I had ignored. Remember that school offers very young children a strange and different place about which to learn.

The middle school student

Moving from primary school to middle school is in some ways easier than the move from middle to secondary school. In fact, a lot of children will stay at the same school for the whole of their 'primary' education. At this stage, children still have only one teacher for all or most of their lessons, and this gives them a sense of continuity. If they do not get on with that one teacher, though, this can be a recipe for trouble. Children of this age are starting to push at the boundaries imposed by adults, and beginning to test exactly how much they can get away with. Puberty is starting at an increasingly young age, and middle school teachers may in fact encounter many of the issues linked to these physical and biochemical changes in their students.

Middle school children start to become more physically imposing, and some of your students may grow much faster than others. It is easy for us to perceive a large, tall child as also being mentally and socially advanced, and to expect better behaviour because we expect them to be generally more mature. Try not to have stereotyped expectations of your children according to their physical appearance.

The secondary school student

Secondary school poses many challenges for young people. Not only do they have to adapt to a totally different environment, but they are also moving into adolescence, a time of vast changes in their physical, mental and emotional make-up. Secondary schools are normally a great deal bigger than the primary or middle school, both in their physical size and in the numbers of students. It is easy for children to get lost in these new surroundings. In addition to this, before they reach secondary school, children may have many preconceptions about bullying, and other horrible things that they think might be in store.

Not only do the students have to deal with all these things;

they also change suddenly from having mainly one teacher for the whole curriculum, to having a different teacher for each subject. They will also be expected to move from room to room for their different lessons. Because secondary school teachers are dealing with large numbers of students, there is not so much opportunity to get to know each child as an individual, and to understand each student's learning needs.

9

TYPES OF
STUDENT

Dealing with different types of student

Every student you teach will be an interesting and complex individual. To an extent, though, it is possible to make some general observations that will help you deal with difficult behaviour. This chapter explores some different types of students, the behaviour problems that they might pose for you, and some of the techniques that you might use to deal with them. Increasingly, the policy of 'inclusion' means that teachers will come across a wide range of different children in mainstream classrooms. Some of these children will have serious behavioural problems that in the past would have been dealt with by a specialist teacher. This is not the place for a discussion about the rights and wrongs of inclusion – we need to address the situation as it is and try to find ways to do our best for all our children.

Special educational needs

The term 'special educational needs' (SEN) has come to encompass a vast range of learning and other difficulties. Although not all special needs are directly connected to behaviour, the repeated misinterpretation of a learning problem could actually lead to a behavioural issue developing over time. If a child finds learning very difficult, it is no surprise that incidents of poor behaviour can occur. As a professional, it is your responsibility to cater for children with all different types of needs, from the most able to the least, from the best behaved to the worst. The more you know about the needs of the students in your class, the better placed you will be to mould your teaching and your teaching style to suit them.

I make no claims to be an expert on special needs, and the advice I give in this chapter is based mainly on my own classroom practice. There will be specialist staff working at your school who have expertise in different types of special need. Make sure you turn to them when you are having problems – they will be only too happy to pass on their knowledge. Some of the most helpful tips I have been given for dealing with individual students have come from talking to the special needs staff who work closely with those children.

Emotional and behavioural difficulties

This is obviously the 'big one' as far as behaviour management is concerned. Students with an emotional or behavioural difficulty may cause problems by being overly confrontational, and unable to control their anger, or they may appear introverted and emotionally fragile. Some of these students will have learned their problematic behaviour through example. Their parents may have had a lack of basic parenting skills, or indeed they may have reacted in a very aggressive, negative way to the child throughout his or her upbringing. On the other hand, some students develop an emotional or behavioural difficulty because of a medical condition.

Dealing with emotional and behavioural difficulties

If you do have a student (or students) with serious emotional or behavioural difficulties in your class, you will need to use all the strategies you have at your disposal to deal with the problem. The case study in this chapter for 'The aggressive/confrontational student' offers some specific ideas for dealing with one particular individual. Here is some general advice:

- Offer a calm, consistent and positive role model from which the student can learn.
- Greet the student by name at the start of the lesson, and mention your positive expectations of what he or she will achieve.
- Be as consistent as is possible about your expectations, but apply flexibility when it proves absolutely necessary.
- Avoid shouting, as this will only exacerbate confrontational behaviour.
- Catch the student behaving well and praise him or her for it. Don't wait for a negative incident to focus on the child.

- Set easily achievable targets for work or behaviour and reward the student for completion of each one.
- Consider seating arrangements – it might be best to seat this child as close to your desk as possible.
- With a particularly aggressive individual, have a back-up plan whereby you can remove yourself and others from danger.

Attention deficit disorder

This is an extreme form of behavioural disturbance, and one that has received much attention in recent times. Students with ADD, or ADHD as it is sometimes called (attention deficit hyperactivity disorder), experience severe problems concentrating on any one activity for any length of time. This might be undertaking a classroom task, or simply staying sitting in their seat. If you do have a child with this condition in your class, you may find that he or she is taking medication, such as Ritalin, to control the problem.

Dealing with ADD

If you do have a student with this disorder in your class, you might find that he or she has a 'statement of special educational needs' which entitles the child to additional support. It could be that an individual helper works with the student in some lessons, or for most of their time at school. The individual case study below on dealing with 'The distracted student' will give you some specific strategies. Here is some general advice:

- As far as possible, ignore minor incidents of misbehaviour from a student with ADD. Focus on the child only when their behaviour is good, using praise as much as you can to encourage repetition of the positive behaviour.
- Find ways to keep your teaching active and varied, so that the child is not asked to sit and listen for long periods of time. Break up longer periods of concentration with practical work.
- Offer the child volunteer tasks that will get him or her out of a seat and involved in a positive and helpful way within the classroom.

127

- Focus exercises may help this student to develop better concentration skills. Look at the exercises explained in the previous chapter – 'Dealing with lack of self-discipline'. Do not, however, expect miracles! A low level of concentration may be all that you can expect from a student with ADD.
- Set small targets throughout the class time that the student can achieve relatively easily. Heap praise on the individual for every task completed.
- Use visual indicators to help the child understand the passing of time. For instance, an individual timetable with coloured symbols, stuck to the desk.
- If the student does become completely distracted, or involved in misbehaviour, try to divert him or her by offering an exciting alternative.

Hyperactivity

Hyperactive children just cannot sit still. This is, of course, a problem in a classroom, where they need to sit still at least some of the time to learn. Hyperactivity can be exacerbated by certain foods and drinks, for instance those with a high sugar or caffeine content. In fact, you may well notice the way in which your students' behaviour changes when they have just had a break, and have consumed sugary canned drinks. The advice given above for dealing with ADD will also be helpful in coping with a hyperactive child.

Learning difficulties

There are a huge range of different learning difficulties – with writing, with spelling, with numbers, and so on. Although a learning difficulty does not necessarily lead to a behavioural one, children can quickly become frustrated and embarrassed by a lack of ability or understanding. If the teacher responds to a learning difficulty in an inappropriate way, for instance by accusing the student of being lazy, then poor behaviour could be the result.

Dealing with learning difficulties

Your job as a teacher is, of course, to cater for the needs of all your class. If a student has a problem such as dyslexia, this will have an impact on the child's learning in many different areas of the curriculum, whenever reading or writing is required. You need to be aware of these learning difficulties, and provide for the individual students in a way that is appropriate to them. Take account of the problems that your children may have throughout the class time, not just when they are working individually. For instance, a child with dyslexia may experience difficulty in recording homework or reading from the board. Again, here is some general advice to help you respond appropriately to the needs of your class:

- Find out exactly what the learning difficulties of your students are, and ask the special needs staff at your school for advice in dealing with them.
- Keep yourself up to date and develop your practice by going on training courses whenever you get the chance. Join an organisation such as NASEN (the National Association for Special Educational Needs – www.nasen.org.uk).
- Whenever possible, use differentiated tasks so that the child with learning difficulties has a chance to succeed. Although differentiating the work is time-consuming, it is important in meeting all your students' needs and can help you avoid misbehaviour.
- Make sure you don't embarrass the student or draw attention to a particular weakness. If you have to talk to a child about a special need, do so in a private, individual way.
- Make some allowances for the difficulty, but keep your standards high. You will not do your children any favours by letting them get away with less than they are capable of achieving.

Special needs staff

There are a wide variety of special needs staff working within the education system, all of whom should be happy to help you deal with the needs of your students. Depending on the size and type of your school, you may have special needs assistants, educational welfare officers, educational psychologists, and so on working with you, either as permanent members of staff, or as visiting consultants. Do make a point of getting to know these staff. Ask them for help, or for more detailed information on an individual who is causing you problems. Talk to them on a regular basis, and remember to let them know how well the advice that they gave you worked.

It could also be that you can assist the special needs team in your school by flagging up students whose needs have not yet been identified. It can be difficult for the special needs staff to spot new cases of special needs, because they do not teach whole classes on a regular basis. Students may develop a behavioural difficulty at any time in their schooling, and you should keep an eye out in your class or classes for students who are experiencing problems, either with their behaviour or with their work.

Some teachers will also have a member of the special needs staff working with them inside the classroom. If this is the case, make sure you plan ahead so that you make the best use of the support teacher's time. Share your lesson plans in advance, and ask for help in adapting the work you are doing so that it best suits those individuals with particular needs. Find out whether the support teacher would prefer to withdraw a few students from the class, to work with on a small group basis, or to work within the classroom, helping integrate the students into the mainstream classroom.

Case studies

The following case studies are entirely fictitious. They are not necessarily about students with special needs, although in each case something is obviously going wrong. In each case study I give an example exploring some of the behavioural issues that you might experience. I also offer a series of suggestions for tackling the behaviour problems. The case studies are set in both the primary and the secondary school, and the tips and suggestions can be adapted to suit your own particular circumstances.

The lazy/poorly motivated student

Cassie just can't seem to be bothered. She rarely completes any work, and if she does finish something, it is scrappy and of poor quality. You are torn between just giving up, letting Cassie get away with producing no work, and confronting her about the problem. When questioned as to why she hasn't completed a task, Cassie will say, 'I couldn't be bothered, Miss.'

You have already tried setting detentions to encourage her to complete the work. Unfortunately, Cassie never turns up for them. This seems to be less a deliberate attempt to avoid the sanction, and more because she actually forgets to come.

Strategies for dealing with the poorly motivated student

- Check with the special needs staff whether Cassie has already been identified as having a learning difficulty. It could be that she is having trouble with writing, or with understanding your lessons. If she has not been tested, ask the special needs team to do this.
- Set Cassie achievable targets during the lesson. For instance, draw a line on the page and ask her to write down to the line in a certain period of time. When (if) she completes each task, give her an instant reward, such as verbal praise or a sticker.
- If your class situation allows, sit with Cassie as she works, talking her through what she needs to do and constantly reinforcing how well she is doing.
- If you are too busy dealing with your class to give Cassie individual attention, sit her with a well-motivated partner who can help and encourage her.

- Find out what really interests Cassie and try to incorporate this into your lesson planning.
- If you have laptops available at your school, try letting Cassie use one. It could be that she is struggling because her writing skills are weak, and that a computer allows her to complete much more work.
- Find out what rewards really motivate Cassie. Perhaps a positive phone call home will do the trick.
- Talk to other members of staff who have taught or who currently teach Cassie. Are they experiencing the same problems? If they are, what strategies do they use? If not, is Cassie only having a problem in your class? If she is, talk to her about why this might be.

The troublemaker

Paul is a nightmare in your lessons! When he does turn up (always late) he immediately disrupts your class by winding the other students up and getting them involved with his misbehaviour. He also acts very aggressively towards the quieter members of the class. He rarely does any work, and when he does complete a task you will find it contains rude, personal comments about you.

When you try to sanction Paul, he responds very negatively, swearing at you and insulting you. He refuses to attend detentions, and will push past you to leave the room if you try to detain him after the lesson.

Strategies for dealing with the troublemaker

- With this serious type of misbehaviour, it is likely that Paul has already been brought to the attention of the special needs team. Check with them about him – is there something specific about his background that you should know? What suggestions do they have for dealing with him, and what is currently being done to help change his behaviour?
- It is probable that the rest of the class are also fed up with Paul. Before he arrives at your lesson, talk to the rest of your

students about what they could do to help you help him improve. For instance, if they can learn to ignore his poor behaviour, he will have less reason to try it on.

- Talk to Paul outside of class time about his behaviour, but be careful not to appear vulnerable when you do this. Simply state what you see to be the problem, and tell him that you are going to sort it out, no matter what it takes. Paul may be used to his teachers giving up on him. Make it clear that you are not about to do this.
- Catch Paul being good (if it ever happens). Public praise might be useful here, especially if this student responds well to peer group approval.
- If Paul does respond so negatively to sanctions, consider whether they are in fact worth using in this situation. Focus instead on positive comments and rewards.
- If you feel it necessary, do not hesitate to bring in a senior member of staff to help you deal with the situation. If it has come to the stage where you feel personally threatened by Paul, or where the rest of the class are picking up on his misbehaviour, it could be that he needs to be removed from your class for a while.
- Talk to other staff about their strategies for dealing with Paul. Perhaps he responds well to a particular teaching style. Does he prefer a 'strict and scary' or a 'firm but fun' approach?
- If you know that his parents or guardians are supportive, phone home and talk to them about his behaviour in your lessons. Be careful, though. From the information in this case study, it could be that his parents act in a similar way, and phoning home might make the situation worse.
- Don't take his behaviour personally, or allow it to make you become defensive. Remember – remain calm and relentlessly polite at all times. Never stoop to his level.
- Try to empathize with Paul and feel sympathy for the serious psychological problems he may have. Aim to feel pity rather than anger when he disrupts your lessons, however hard this might be.

The distracted student

Jenna is a lovely child, but she does find it very hard to stay focused on anything. In the mornings it takes her a long time to sit down and settle on the carpet for you to take the register. When you set a task, she will generally start off very well, but after a few minutes she will have become distracted, chatting to her friends, wandering around the room, or simply staring out of the window, lost to the world.

When you challenge her about this, she will either promise to go back to work (but fail to), or become upset and run out of the classroom. You have tried various tactics, such as ignoring low-level misbehaviour, or setting her targets to complete, but nothing seems to work. You are concerned that your relationship with Jenna is degenerating.

Strategies for dealing with the distracted student

- Check with the special needs staff to see whether Jenna has a specific learning difficulty. If she does, find ways to differentiate the work for her.
- Pay Jenna personal attention when she arrives in the morning, giving her a positive experience of school right from the word go. Greet her by name and tell her how much you are looking forward to her working well for you that day. Repeat this greeting after break and lunchtimes.
- Jenna clearly has difficulties getting her mind focused first thing in the mornings. Give her an 'adult' role at the start of the day to ensure that she has a target the moment she arrives at school. For instance, she might be responsible for setting out the class resources, or even for ensuring that the rest of the children are seated on the carpet ready for registration.
- Look carefully at your lesson planning and ensure that you are not asking the class to listen for extended periods or to focus on one task for a long time. Divide the work up into short activities and set time limits for each one, giving rewards and praise for completion of each task.
- Ensure that Jenna fully understands the tasks that you set.

After the class has started work, go and sit with her for a while to check that she knows what she is meant to do, or ask a teaching assistant or other member of support staff to do this.

- Set Jenna achievable targets and make sure that you check up on how she is getting on at regular intervals during the activity. Reward her (with whatever reward best motivates her) for every little thing that she achieves.
- Find Jenna a responsible partner or friend with whom she works well, and ask the helper to assist in keeping Jenna on task.
- Use an egg timer to give Jenna a visual aid for staying on task. Set her tasks that will take one run-through of the sand. Ask her to raise her hand every time the sand runs out, and go to check up on her.
- Find out what Jenna enjoys outside of class time. If she is keen on drawing, give her plenty of art-based tasks. Encourage a positive feeling of success by capitalizing on her talents, for example asking Jenna to help you put up some displays.
- Get in touch with Jenna's parents or carers and have a chat with them. Build up a team approach, suggesting ways in which they can support you in improving Jenna's learning behaviour.

The student with social problems

Sally is a strange child. You see her wandering around the school alone at break and lunchtimes, looking very sorry for herself. She arrives in the morning smelling and looking dirty, and the other children are beginning to tease her about this. Although her individual work is good, she is unable to work well in a group situation. In fact, none of the other children want to work with her, because her behaviour is odd. This is putting you in an awkward position, because confrontations arise within the class when you try to make them accept her into group activities.

When you talk to Sally individually, she refuses to look you in the eye, and mumbles her answers so that you can hardly hear her. It doesn't seem fair to sanction Sally, because she is not actually doing anything wrong, but the strangeness of her behaviour is having an impact on your class as a whole.

Dealing with the problem

- From the evidence given here, it sounds as though Sally should be brought to the attention of the child protection officer, or the educational welfare services, if this has not already been done. Go and talk to the special needs staff and find out about Sally's background and home situation.
- Try to avoid the necessity for group work, at least for a while. If you do set a group task, find a way for Sally to complete the task individually, but without making her seem like the odd one out.
- Build up Sally's confidence, perhaps by praising her with written comments on a good piece of work. Take care that the rest of the class do not witness the praise, as they may use this as a further reason to isolate her.
- Spend some time talking to Sally individually, gradually winning her trust and getting her to learn how to make eye contact, and talk more clearly. Coax her gently, asking her to look you in the eye while you talk to her.
- If the situation with your class seems to warrant it, talk to them without Sally being present. Point out how important it is to accept anybody and everybody when working in a group. Without mentioning Sally by name, ask them to imagine how horrible it must feel to be left out of a group because nobody likes you.
- Do some whole-class PSHE work on bullying and friendship issues. Make it completely clear to the children that you will not accept any incidents of bullying in your class. Talk about suitable sanctions for those who do bully.
- See if you can find one or two members of the class who might be able to befriend Sally. Try putting Sally in a pair with one of these students to help her learn some social skills.
- Ask Sally whether she would like to stay in at break and lunchtimes on occasions, when you need help with a classroom task. (You could also ask for some other volunteers to work alongside her, in the hope that friendships might arise.) Sally might help you sort resources, or put up a display. This will help make her feel wanted and important, and could

assist in boosting her confidence. It will also stop her feeling lonely and isolated during break times.

The aggressive/confrontational student

Les is a real problem around the school, and other teachers frequently refer to his aggressive and antisocial behaviour in their classes. He is a large, well-built boy, and you often feel physically threatened by him. At the slightest provocation, Les starts to shout and cause problems. He acts very negatively towards the other members of the class, and they are becoming scared of him.

Les rarely does any work in class, but when you try to sanction him about this he reacts in a hostile manner. On one recent occasion, Les picked up a chair and threatened to throw it at you.

Dealing with the aggressive/confrontational student

- Les clearly has a problem with managing his anger. Again, check that his special needs have been identified and evaluated. Find out from the special needs staff exactly what it is that 'sets him off' and how to avoid exacerbating his aggression.
- Suggest to the special needs staff (or to the school management) that Les be given some anger management classes. Make it clear that there are a number of members of staff who feel threatened by his behaviour.
- Avoid confronting Les at all costs – it is not worth the risk to your own safety to do so, and confrontation is apparently what makes Les aggressive. Instead, try to remain calm and use low-key approaches.
- Create a 'get-out' option for Les. For example, when he feels he is going to blow, he could leave the room rather than allowing the situation to develop. Find somewhere safe for him to go in these circumstances, for instance to sit outside the school office.
- It is possible that people are reacting to Les's size and physical

137

presence and expecting him to cause trouble. Try to avoid focusing on Les and the problems he creates in your classroom. Only concentrate on him when he is doing something right.

- Ask other staff for advice about dealing with Les, and talk your fears through with a more senior teacher. Explain to them exactly how you feel, and how Les makes other members of the class feel. It is probable that Les's behaviour has already come to the attention of the headteacher, and that he has been warned or even excluded in the past.

- Ensure that you document all the incidents involving Les, especially when aggressive or violent behaviour is threatened or used. Pass on copies of this information to managers and the special needs staff. If you feel the situation is getting out of hand, and you are actually in danger of being assaulted, discuss the issue with a senior manager or union representative.

10

WHAT THE
STUDENTS SAID

In writing this book I conducted interviews with a range of students, to find out their views on behaviour. The students were very clear and often extremely perceptive about how their teachers can make them behave. Some of their comments surprised me – perhaps reflecting a gap between teacher and student perceptions of misbehaviour.

The students represented a cross-section of a secondary school community, and were from a range of age groups, cultural and social backgrounds. I spoke to students who were generally well behaved in lessons, and also to those who were typically poorly behaved. The students had a wide range of different abilities, some very able, and others with specific learning difficulties.

Classroom control

'What makes a teacher good at controlling a class?'

The students identified two types of teachers who were good at controlling their behaviour. The first kind could be described as 'firm but fun': the students liked this teacher, but he or she could also keep them in line. The second could be described as 'strict and scary': although the students behaved well, they did not really enjoy the lessons, and they felt that the teacher did not actually like the class. Here are some aspects of the two teaching styles described by the students:

The 'firm but fun' teacher
- *Teaching style:* This teacher was firm with the class right from the first lesson, telling the class what was expected, rather than asking them. (The students described how some teachers 'pleaded' with them to behave.) This teacher demonstrated his or her expectations constantly, for instance sorting out the students' uniform before letting them into the classroom. If necessary, this type of teacher would shout, but could also be 'nice', 'funny' and 'like a mum'.
- *The work:* This teacher made the lessons and the work seem interesting, so that the students had fun while they were

learning. The teacher might play some games, perhaps at the beginning and end of the lesson. The learning was varied and the students were not asked to work in total silence. They were clear about how much work they needed to do to satisfy this teacher. If the lesson was hard, this teacher would reward the class for their additional efforts. It was felt important that they were not asked to do tasks beyond their capabilities. There was a very clear correlation between the students liking a teacher and liking the subject he or she taught.

- *Discipline:* The students knew very clearly that this kind of teacher would give sanctions, but this was done in a calm and controlled way. If it was necessary to give a 'whole class' sanction, such as a detention, the teacher would let the good students leave first, so that they were not punished for the misbehaviour of others.
- *Relationship with the students:* The students liked and respected this teacher – the teacher was described as happy and 'alive'. They could relate to this teacher because he or she personalized the work and was happy to chat openly with them. They felt that this teacher actually liked them, and was always welcoming to the class.
- *Students' perception of the teacher:* This sort of teacher had a good reputation within the school, and this was probably quite an important factor in student expectations and behaviour. They were aware that this teacher had both a 'good' and a 'bad' side and they were wary of getting on the wrong side of him/her.

The 'strict and scary' teacher

- *Teaching style:* The students said that this teacher was more likely to be male than female, with a strong, deep voice. One student commented that 'everyone does their work but they don't like this teacher'.
- *The work:* The students had to complete their work before they were allowed to leave the classroom. At times, the students felt they were too scared of this teacher to ask for help.
- *Discipline:* This teacher used the threat of sanctions to discipline the class, and was also keen on giving out detentions. The teacher always followed up on detentions

and, if necessary, would actually come to collect the student to ensure that the sanction was served. The students had to line up in silence before entering the classroom. This teacher often used a seating plan as a form of control – for instance seating the students boy/girl alternately.

- *Relationship with the students:* The students used the word 'threaten' quite frequently in association with this teacher. They did not feel that they could develop a close relationship with this teacher.
- *Students' perception of the teacher:* Apparently, this teacher 'looks like they're not scared of the students'. The teacher was given the respect of the students, but through fear rather than admiration.

'What makes a teacher bad at controlling a class?'

Again, the students were extremely clear about what teachers did or did not do that might make a class misbehave. Much of what they said referred to the students' perception of the teacher's state of mind. There seemed to be a substantial gap between what this type of teacher *said* they would do, and what they actually *did* do.

- *Teaching style:* This kind of teacher 'acts as though they're scared of the kids'. The students found this hard to explain fully, but they certainly knew when it was happening. They also identified the feeling that the teacher didn't want to get on the wrong side of the children. Many of the students explained that this type of teacher 'shouts, but isn't strict', or is 'always shouting' and 'having a go at you'.
- *The work:* The students misbehaved if the teaching was not fun, and if the teacher didn't explain things properly. With some teachers they did one type of work all the time, and this meant they became bored and subsequently misbehaved.
- *Discipline:* This type of teacher used the threat of sanctions but didn't follow it through, either because the sanction was never actually applied, or because it was not chased up once given. Alternatively, the teacher used the ultimate sanction every

lesson (for instance sending a student out), becoming over-defensive and giving excessive punishments, which the students felt was very unfair.

The students explained that some teachers started off by being lenient with the class, then if the students misbehaved they 'pleaded' with them to behave, rather than 'telling' them to. The teacher typically allowed the students to sit where they wanted, rather than using a seating plan. He or she was also defensive – likely to scream at the students before they had a chance to explain what was going on.

- *Relationship with the students:* The students wanted to be treated as equals, and disliked teachers who talked down to them, or who gave the impression that 'you're not as good as them'.
- *Students' perception of the teacher:* The students felt frustrated by teachers who could not control them. One comment was that 'some teachers bring it on themselves'. Another student commented that sometimes the class would not even give a teacher a chance, perhaps because he or she was new, young, or inexperienced. There was also a strong feeling that some ineffective teachers had favourites, or treated boys and girls differently. The less well-behaved students felt that this teacher might 'pick on' them, having a go at one individual in particular.

'Describe your ideal teacher'

Of course, there is not necessarily a correlation between what students see as their 'ideal' teacher, and a teacher who is good at controlling behaviour. However, the students were very clear that they wanted their teachers to be able to control the class, only they wanted this to be done in a particular way. When asked the question about their ideal teacher, all the students described someone who would fit very closely under the 'firm but fun' style of teaching.

- *Teaching style:* Words such as 'funny' and 'nice' came up frequently. An ideal teacher had a 'bubbly personality' and made everything fun, for instance playing with words to make the work more interesting. It was important for teachers to be 'happy not grumpy', and to have very few 'bad days'. The ideal teacher was fairly strict, with the ability to be serious when necessary.

- *The work:* The work was made fun and interesting, with lots of rewards. The lessons were varied, sometimes easy and definitely not always writing, preferably with some games included. The teacher would always help the students when they needed it.
- *Discipline:* Although this mythical 'perfect teacher' could be strict when the class behaved badly, he or she did not shout. The students said that the teacher should respond to the way that the class is behaving, becoming strict if needed, but staying 'fun' otherwise. The teacher should also give the students a chance before handing out detentions.
- *Relationship with the students:* Again, the students were very firm about wanting to be treated as equals, and indeed why not? They also wanted the teacher to have proper conversations with them.
- *Students' perception of the teacher:* The students felt that they would get to know this type of teacher well. The 'ideal teacher' is firm, but fun, and they would soon develop a good personal relationship with him or her.

Rewards and sanctions

'What rewards work and why?'

The students were surprisingly unimpressed by the majority of rewards given at school. Probably the main 'reward' they actually experienced, perhaps without properly realizing it, was verbal or written praise from a teacher they respected. The students were impressively materialistic, suggesting that decent and tangible rewards would be far more likely to make them behave! Happily, some of the most well-motivated students identified the more subtle reward of a good education.

Merits/commendations
Younger students were keen on collecting merits, but pointed out that it was mainly the 'good kids' who wanted them, and they were therefore not particularly useful as a form of control. Some of the less well-behaved students were honest enough to admit that, as they kept losing their diaries (where merits were noted), they had nowhere to collect them.

Merits were less effective if you didn't actually get anything in return. The students suggested that, if you received points for merits which could be 'cashed in' for prizes, they would be much more effective. The students also pointed out that some teachers forgot to give merits. Other teachers 'glazed over' the good, quiet children in the class, only handing them out to those students who were loud and noisy.

Awards evening/certificates
For those students with supportive parents who were proud of their achievements, certificates were viewed as a very popular reward. The students suggested that certificates should be given as publicly as possible, for instance in assembly, so that the reward seemed more tangible.

Other suggestions for rewards
The students wanted tangible rewards for good behaviour. They liked the idea of 'desk duty', running errands for the office and for teachers (and missing lessons as a result – a very popular option). Another popular tangible reward was badges, or prizes such as Mars bars and cans of Coke. What a materialistic bunch we teach!

'What punishments work and why?

The students had strong views on how efficient the various sanctions were at making them (and their peers) behave. Overall, they felt that the majority of punishments were useful for the 'good' students, who actually wanted to succeed. However, they felt that many sanctions were ineffective for the 'bad' students, because they didn't care (or pretended not to care) about being punished.

Detentions

The students had mixed feelings about detentions. Depending on why they were given, and how they were run, they felt that they were either a useful method of punishment, or else a complete waste of time. Some students said that they didn't turn up to detentions, because there was no real pressure to do so. Others said that if they understood *why* the detention was given, they would turn up for it.

Another point that students made was that they sometimes felt they were being punished for needing help. Clearly, in one case, a teacher had given a detention for lack of work during class time. However, the student perceived the detention as a punishment for lack of ability. Whole-class detentions were seen as being extremely unfair.

Short detentions were viewed as an effective method of punishment, but long detentions were generally disliked. Detentions given at break and lunchtime could cause problems for the students, as they then had no time to eat. In fact, I have experienced the difficulties that this can cause myself; when a student misbehaves in a lesson directly after a break-time detention, because of hunger, or low energy levels. The students felt strongly that the teacher should set them work to do during a detention, or some type of community sanction, such as picking up rubbish. They suggested that this could then lead to a shortened detention.

Being sent out/taken off timetable

The 'red card' system, where a student is removed from the classroom, was viewed as a good punishment, mainly because it got the very difficult students out of lessons and allowed the others to continue with their work uninterrupted. The students were also aware that such a high-level punishment went on school records. However, they felt that being sent out of a lesson did not have much of an impact on the behaviour of the 'bad' students, because it was viewed as a big joke. (It could be, of course, that these students played down their embarrassment at being given a severe sanction by making a joke out of it.) Taking a student off the normal timetable because he or she had misbehaved was also viewed as a bit 'stupid'. It was felt that the student had then achieved exactly the desired result – to get out of lessons and avoid doing any work!

Exclusion

The majority of the students did not expect ever to be excluded. However, they had firm views about how exclusion was seen by those who did merit such a severe sanction. While they did feel that exclusion helped create a climate for better behaviour in their lessons, I was surprised to find that they also felt exclusion would mean 'a day off school to do what you want' for the most poorly behaved students in a school.

Other forms of sanction

The students felt that being put on report was a very useful sanction, particularly if they had to report to a teacher at lunchtime. They also suggested that it would be useful to have a meeting with the teacher, the parents and the head if a student was consistently misbehaving. Phone calls and letters home were seen to work if the parents of the student were supportive. Many of the students said that they did try to avoid this particular sanction.

Other factors affecting behaviour

'What effect does the classroom environment have on your behaviour?'

The students felt that if a classroom was already scruffy, they would be far more likely to drop litter on the floor. If, on the other hand, the class environment was bright and colourful, this made them want to keep it that way. Some of the students felt that the rooms they were taught in were 'dull' and 'cold'. If this was the case, they were less than happy about working in these rooms, and more likely to misbehave as a result.

'What subjects do you find it easiest to behave in?'

Unsurprisingly, perhaps, the students felt it was easiest to behave in the non-academic subjects, such as art, music and PE. They explained that these areas of the curriculum needed less concentration, and they felt more relaxed during the lessons. PE in particular was seen as being a fun lesson rather than a work lesson. The students also felt it was easy to behave during form or tutor time. This was partly because they knew the other members of their form well, and thus felt relaxed. In addition, form time was seen as different to lesson time, because they were not expected to work.

Student thoughts on misbehaviour

'What do you feel about students whose behaviour is very poor?'

The students had mixed feelings about poorly behaved students. Superficially, they found such students funny, and felt that they added interest to the lessons. Worryingly, they also saw a clear relationship between poor behaviour and being popular. The majority of students did not feel personally threatened by the badly behaved people at their school.

However, feelings of annoyance were also voiced. The students felt that these children took all the teacher's attention, and they said this was not fair. They also offered feelings of sympathy for teachers who were faced with difficult behaviour. There was a strong sense that these poorly behaved students should not be allowed to affect adversely the education of others.

Some of the students mentioned that they had been called 'boffins' by the less well-behaved members of the school, because they actually wanted to behave properly. This name-calling was, however, viewed with derision, particularly by the older students. These students said such insults were motivated by jealousy, because they wanted to work hard and get a good job. The students also said that there was a tendency for the boys to call the girls 'boffins'.

'Why do students misbehave?'

The students were very perceptive about why their fellow students misbehaved. They identified the 'ringleaders' whose example they would follow because they were scared not to. In addition, these ringleaders were seen as being popular members of the class, and being popular was viewed as a very important attribute. The students explained that they would follow the 'bad kids' because those people were loud, daring and willing to challenge the teachers. Often, this misbehaviour would seem funny to the class, and they would therefore want to 'have a go' too, to see what effect they could create. If their friends were 'mucking about', the students explained that this would make them feel more confident about joining in.

The students identified boredom as a key factor in creating misbehaviour. By messing around, they would get attention, both from the teacher and from the rest of the class. In this way, they would look 'hard' in front of their friends and create a distraction from boring work. Another problem was an inability to control themselves. This lack of self-discipline was stronger at particular times of the day and week, or after particular lessons, such as PE. The idea of 'gangs' also came up. Those students who were unwilling to join a gang in poor behaviour expressed the fear that the others might become violent towards them, or turn people against them.

'Describe a poorly behaved student'

When asked to describe students with poor behaviour, the interviewees listed a number of characteristics:

- They 'backchatted' to teachers, talking rudely when their behaviour was challenged.
- They made a big deal out of being given a sanction, even when they had earned it.

- They enjoyed showing off, and wanted to get their own way all the time.
- If they didn't get their own way, they might walk out of the class.
- They 'acted hard' in lessons.
- They were willing to swear, both at other students and at the teacher.
- They didn't care about learning, perhaps because neither they nor their parents cared about getting qualifications.
- They were likely to smoke outside lesson time.
- They were also likely to be identified as a bully by other students.

In addition, the students mentioned some more 'positive' aspects related to poorly behaved students:

- They got respect from their peers.
- They were more likely to get the teacher's attention.
- They were more likely to be popular within the peer group.

'What should be done about poorly behaved students?'

This question seemed to leave the students rather stumped. One suggestion was that there should be special schools for 'naughty' children. This would be a good idea, they said, because it would allow the people who wanted to work to get on with it. (Clearly, these students held no truck with the concept of inclusion!) A second idea was that the 'ringleaders' should get 'taken out' (by whatever method) early on. If this happened in the first year at school, the peer group would be better behaved, because they would not have picked up on how 'rewarding' misbehaviour could be.

'Do you behave well? If so, why?'

Those students who answered 'yes' had a strong motivation (usually from home) to succeed. Parental influence was cited as a very important factor, along with older brothers and sisters who had gone to university. These students were not afraid to stand out from the crowd, or to be termed 'boffins', because they knew it was OK to be smart. They wanted to do well, and get the best education they possibly could, because that way they could get the job they wanted.

Part Four

THE WIDER
ENVIRONMENT

11

THE
CLASSROOM

The classroom environment

Think for a moment about the way the spaces we live in affect the way that we feel. For instance, if you live in a small flat with several other people, you may find yourself becoming stressed and losing your temper easily. People start to get under each other's feet and feelings run high. Similarly, if you live or work in a cluttered and untidy environment, you are likely to feel depressed and mentally 'overcrowded' as well. If, on the other hand, you are lucky enough to live or work in an open, spacious, light and airy space, with a wonderful view, you are likely to spend your time there in a much more positive mood, and consequently you will live or work in a more effective and more relaxed way.

The way that you as a teacher use space, and also the way that your classroom is set up, will have a huge impact on the behaviour of your students. In Chapter 5 – 'Teaching styles' – I looked at the ways in which teachers can use the space to improve behaviour. This chapter looks at how the physical environment of the classroom can be used and improved to have a positive impact on behaviour. In addition to helping you control the behaviour of your students, your classroom should also help *you* stay calm, happy and relaxed.

From the moment they first arrive at your room, your students will be making judgements (probably subconsciously) about what to expect from you as a teacher, simply by what they first see of you and your space. You want to create the feeling that you are in control of this environment, so that your students view you as being 'in charge'. While there is much about our classrooms that we cannot change – for instance, their shape, their size, and often their general condition – there are also many ways that we can improve how our rooms look and consequently the behaviour of our students within them.

Please note: I use the term 'classroom' in this chapter to describe the whole range of different teaching spaces – from rooms to halls, from drama studios to gymnasiums.

Improving the classroom environment

Your students need to perceive your room as a safe, calm environment where learning is going to take place. If you teach in the primary sector, this is the place where your children are going to be spending the majority of each day, and it should therefore be as welcoming, comfortable and well organized as possible. Similarly, if you teach in the secondary sector, this is the place where *you* are going to be spending the majority of your time, and each class that visits you there should find you in control of a wonderful 'haven of learning'. Here are some ideas for improving your classroom environment:

- *Keep it tidy:* A tidy environment will help you create a tidy style in your teaching. It will also give your students the perception of order and structure. When we are surrounded by clutter, it is much harder to work, for instance if we need to find a specific piece of equipment. Try to keep all your resources – files, folders, pens, etc. – in one area, so that the room looks tidy at first sight.
- *Keep it organized:* In the primary classroom, resources for many different subjects need to be stored. It is very useful to set up 'stations' for different resources, and then train your children so they know where to go to get a particular item. In a secondary classroom you might have a specific place where your students store textbooks and exercise books. Your lesson can start with students retrieving their learning materials, or with volunteers handing out the books.
- *Clarify the different areas:* In the primary classroom, different subjects might be taught in different parts of the space (an area for music, a place for art, an area for role play, and so on). Make a clear divide between these different spaces to help you control the children, particularly if they work on a number of subjects at one time. The divide could be physical, using different colours, types of floor covering or screens. You might use signs and displays to show where the various activities take place, and where related resources are stored. If secondary teachers have the space, they can also use this

idea of different 'zones'. For instance, in an English classroom there could be an area for silent reading, another for dictionary and spelling work, another for writing, and so on.

- *Keep it safe:* Ensure that your classroom environment is safe – particularly if you work with challenging students. Keep those dangerous chemicals or sharp scissors out of the way. Have clear rules about bags and other equipment at the start of lessons, a time when safety issues often arise. Of course, your classroom needs to be a safe environment for you as well. If you do have any concerns, there should be a named health and safety representative at your school.

- *Make it fun and colourful:* Interesting displays can really add to the feeling of a good, positive classroom environment. Displays are also a very effective learning tool, and a good way of celebrating your students' achievements. See the following section – 'Some thoughts on displays' – for more advice.

- *Create an engaging atmosphere:* Music, lights, sound and costumes can all help you create a more engaging atmosphere in your classroom. Our students turn up at their lessons expecting to be greeted by a relatively dull and unimaginative space in which to work. If we challenge this expectation once in a while, we will encourage interest, focus and a stronger sense of engagement with the work.

- *Personalize the space:* You will spend a lot of time in your room, and you want your students to view it as your space. Why not, then, bring a few personal touches into the room? If you love plants, add some greenery; if you're an animal lover, introduce a class pet. This is a great way of educating your children about taking responsibility, and might be used as a reward for good behaviour.

- *Think carefully about the layout:* The way you set out the desks in your room will say a great deal about your teaching style, and will have an impact on student behaviour. See the section in this chapter on 'Classroom layout' for some more ideas.

Some thoughts on displays

No matter how poor the general condition of your classroom, you can always cheer it up with displays. In fact, it might be that you can use displays as a good way of covering up dirty walls or peeling paint. However, do not simply view your displays as 'wallpaper' – they must be worthy of their place on your walls. Displays can aid your students' learning, and are an excellent reward for good work. Here are some thoughts about effective use of displays.

- *Make them interesting:* You might use a variety of bright colours on each display, or stick to two colours for a two-tone effect. You could create a three-dimensional display related to a current topic, for instance with 3-D fireworks flying across your wall at the time of fireworks night. Don't forget the ceiling as well as a place for displays – tie a piece of string across your room to hang up the students' work.
- *Make them interactive:* Encourage your students to interact with displays. You could put big questions on the wall, related to the topic you are studying, then give the students Post-it notes to write up their answers. You might have 'lift up' flaps for the students to look under.
- *Keep them tidy:* Caring for displays demonstrates respect for the students and their work. Replace drawing pins regularly, tidy up any ripped corners, or change the display as soon as it becomes tired.
- *Change them regularly:* If you simply stick up a load of displays at the start of the year, then run out of steam, your students will cease to notice them. Try to find time to refresh them every few weeks.
- *Relate them to the learning:* Use displays to applaud your students' current attainment and the work that is happening at the moment. This helps reinforce the positive work and learning that takes place in your classroom, and consequently encourages good behaviour.
- *Learn to delegate:* In some schools, additional staff are now available to help with creating displays. The students can also

be involved – this helps motivate them and lessens the burden on the teacher. Children tend to have more respect for work done by their peers, and will probably take better care of displays created by classmates. You can sit back and act as 'art director'.

Classroom layout

Classroom layout has a strong effect on students' behaviour and learning, and on their perceptions of what will happen inside the room. Depending on your age range and the subject(s) you teach, you might have to decide how to set out desks and chairs, or stools and lab benches, or perhaps a whole range of furniture in the primary classroom. You might also change the classroom layout for different types of work, getting the children to help you move furniture about. Here are some thoughts about how the students might perceive different classroom layouts, and also their possible impact on learning and behaviour. The examples given use the most common type of classroom furniture; desks and chairs.

The desks in rows

This is perceived as a traditional way of setting up a classroom, both by teachers and by students. It can feel like a safe option for the teacher who is having trouble controlling the behaviour of his or her class.

Advantages: The students are all facing forwards, and it is therefore relatively easy for the teacher to spot off-task chatter or low-level misbehaviour. The students can all see the board, and resources, books, etc., can easily be passed along the rows. This layout also makes it easier to draw up a seating plan.

Disadvantages: It is difficult to do group work with the desks set out this way. There can be a tendency for the teacher to ignore students at the ends of each row, simply because they are out of the line of sight. This set-up favours the 'chalk and talk' method of teaching, with teacher-led lessons. When moving round the class, the teacher can only work with one pair of students at a time.

The desks in groups

This generally encourages a more modern style of teaching, where exploration and group work take place among the students. For a teacher with a difficult class, this style of layout can be a source of problems, because it can be harder to control behaviour.

Advantages: Group activities can take place easily, and the class work is more likely to be student based. The teacher can talk to a whole group at a time, and it is likely that he or she will move more freely around the room during the lesson.

Disadvantages: If the teacher cannot see all the faces, the students could get away with chatting and plotting misbehaviour more easily. It can be harder for the students to see the board. The students may view the teacher as less traditional, or less strict, and this perception could also lead to behaviour problems.

Some thoughts on different spaces

Teachers work in a huge range of different spaces, depending on both the age range that they teach and the subject or subjects in which they specialize. Teachers in a primary or middle school will work mainly within one space (their classroom), but they could also spend time in other places within the school. They might work in the school gym to teach PE, or outside in the nature area for a science lesson. Secondary school teachers are more likely to be restricted to one room (or several different rooms if they are not lucky enough to have their own teaching space). However, even secondary teachers will at times have the desire or opportunity to move from their normal space to a different one, for instance measuring the school playground in a maths lesson.

Each of the spaces within a school has its own natural advantages and disadvantages when it comes to behaviour management. If we wish to maximize our control over our students' behaviour, we need to be aware of these positive and negative aspects of the spaces in which we work. The ideas below should help you understand these features, and help you exploit the advantages of your own space or spaces, and minimize the difficulties that you might encounter.

The classroom

When dealing with problem behaviour, the classroom space has many advantages. The fixed nature of the seating and desks (and carpets or other areas in the primary classroom) gives a strong sense of control for teacher and students. Once the class are seated, there is little opportunity for them to move around, and consequently less chance of physical disruptions. From the front of the room, the teacher can generally see all the students' faces, to ensure that the students are concentrating fully and behaving sensibly.

On the downside, students seated at desks are physically restricted, and may look for alternative outlets for their energy, particularly if they are restless, kinaesthetically inclined, or if they lack concentration and self-discipline. Some students may rock back on their chairs, others might create disruption through excessive noise or poor behaviour, perhaps throwing things across the room. Students who find it difficult to sit still may get up and wander around the room. The room could also be fairly cramped if it is small and has a large number of desks and chairs.

Maximizing the advantages

Make it a priority to keep your students in their seats, particularly if you are having problems with behaviour. Make it clear that 'stay seated at all times' is a very important rule. Train your students to raise their hands and wait if they need help, and come to them in the order that their hands went up. If a child does need to leave his or her seat, insist that permission is asked first.

Talk with your children about how you want them to sit

(whether on a chair or on a carpet). Students who are unable to sit still can be a source of stress and annoyance for the teacher. You'll find some useful tips about teaching good 'sitting behaviour' in Chapter 13.

Consider the layout of your desks: rows facing the front is probably the preferred method for a difficult class. When you address the class as a whole, look around to ensure that all faces are turned towards you, and that each student is attentive and ready to listen.

Minimizing the difficulties

If you teach a particularly restless individual, set 'staying in your seat' as a target, rewarding the child if he or she manages to achieve this target throughout the lesson. Give other outlets for physical energy, for instance some pipe cleaners to twist into shapes. Make sure that your lessons include opportunities for active, practical work as well as more sedate activities.

You might have a brief 'movement' time, perhaps when students are gathering materials for their work. Agree a signal, such as clapping your hands, for when you want them to return to their seats. If you use movement time with a tricky class, try allowing only one or two groups to be on the go at any one time. Where the lesson time is particularly long, consider incorporating some 'break out' times at various points during the session.

The science lab

Science rooms can be very exciting places for students, with interesting equipment to use, and fascinating experiments to try out. Science teachers in a secondary school will often have the services of a lab technician to help them prepare materials for their lessons. It is likely that the lab benches will be in a fixed position within the space (probably facing the front), and this means that students cannot cause disruption by moving the furniture around. With benches facing the front of the room, it is easy for the teacher to demonstrate practical experiments to the class.

161

On the other hand, science laboratories have many potential dangers. Safety issues must be at the forefront of the teacher's mind, and if you are teaching difficult students, it may be tempting to avoid practical work because of the possible hazards. Labs may also have sinks, taps and Bunsen burners, which could prove appealing to less sensible students.

Maximizing the advantages

Try not to shy away from practical work if you teach in a lab. This is just the type of lesson that students see as fun and interesting. It is only through experience that they can learn how to conduct experiments in a safe and sensible way. It could be that you have to suffer a few very stressful practical lessons before your students are properly trained in using the equipment. Again, make sure your class is facing the front, looking at you, and concentrating fully, before you address them. You could use the reward of being allowed to do a practical experiment to ensure that you have the class's full attention while you demonstrate exactly what they have to do.

Minimizing the difficulties

Keep temptation away from your students, as far as you can. Lock any dangerous chemicals, or tools, in a cupboard, or keep them in another room. Make it clear right from the start that you will not stand for students messing around with taps and Bunsen burners, and that to do so would be to incur an immediate sanction. Consider spending initial lessons training the students in lab safety, making posters to display on the walls to remind them of the rules.

'Open' spaces

Open spaces, such as the drama studio, the gymnasium, or the hall, can be wonderful environments for learning. Your students have a greater degree of freedom to move around in an open space, and they are less likely to feel restricted and restless.

Lessons that take place in these spaces tend to be those that students enjoy. They are also generally less academic areas of the curriculum. There is less focus on activities such as writing and book learning, which can lead to disruptive behaviour.

However, the sight of a big, open space may offer your students an overwhelming temptation to run around. It can prove difficult to pull the class back together into one part of the space. There may be high levels of noise during the lesson, making it difficult for the teacher to regain the children's attention. If the teacher does want to do written work, it may be hard to access chairs, desks and materials. Students may resent being asked to write in practical subjects, because they don't see them as involving this kind of work.

Maximizing the advantages

From the first time that you meet your students in an open space, make it clear that the work will be fun and full of excitement. However, make it perfectly apparent too that they will need to develop a high degree of control and self-discipline to enjoy your lessons properly. You could use the threat of not doing a practical lesson as a form of control over students who lack self-discipline. If they want to have fun, they *must* learn to work in partnership with you and follow the rules.

Minimizing the difficulties

Be very clear about expected behaviour within the space, right from the start. You could perhaps line the class up outside the room and tell them that when they are allowed in, they must immediately sit on the floor (in a circle or in a group) so that you can start your lesson. If they fail to follow this instruction, take them back outside and line them up again, explaining to them that they are wasting their fun lesson time. Find a good way of gaining the class's attention within your open space, for instance one of the silence commands described in Chapter 3 (see 'Wait for silence').

There are various options for approaching written work. You

could set all written tasks for homework, and only allow the students to do a practical lesson if their homework is complete. Another alternative is to split the lessons up into a practical session followed by a writing time. If you do not have any desks and chairs in your room, you could ask the students to sit on the floor and write on clipboards, or you could find an empty classroom that is more conducive to written work.

Teaching outdoors

Just as with working in an open space, teaching outdoors offers a wonderful sense of freedom for your students. They will also see it as something out of the ordinary, a chance to escape from the school building and explore the wider environment. Even if you teach a very academic subject, do find some opportunities to take your class outside.

The advantages and disadvantages of working outside are very similar to the 'open space' example given above. Remember – explain your behaviour requirements to the class before they enter the space. If you don't do this, you will find it very difficult to regain their attention. Similarly, agree some sort of silence command with the class.

The teacher within the space

The way that the teacher uses the teaching space plays an important part in achieving control of behaviour. Your students will look at the way you set up the room, and the way that you move within it, to help them make decisions about how to behave. Find lots of ways to mark this as *your* territory: a space where you are in charge, and where positive, exciting things are going to happen. Establishing this feeling is particularly important in your first few lessons with a class. Here are some suggestions as to how you might do it:

- Meet the students outside the space, greeting them on your own terms rather than on theirs.

- Create a physical barrier between the class and the room, by positioning yourself in front of the door.
- Ensure appropriate behaviour before you allow them into the room, making your expectations clear.
- As you allow the students in, greet them in a positive manner, using first names if you can.
- If another teacher has used this room previously, give some clear visual indicators that it is now your space. For instance, put up some striking displays of your own, or change the layout around.
- Don't get stuck at the front – move around the space in a dynamic way, visiting all the students during the course of the lesson.
- On occasions, change the way that your room is laid out, for instance moving the desks into a U shape for a debate. An element of surprise is useful to keep a class on its toes.
- Sometimes, use the space in an unusual way. Sit on your desk rather than standing in front of it, or stand at the back of the room to read a piece of text.
- Watch that you don't direct more of your teaching to one side of the room (typically to the right if you are right-handed).
- Use the vertical as well as the horizontal space – move up and down as well as side to side. Crouch down beside students to chat, ask them to sit on the floor to hear a story, or stand on a desk to declaim a poem to your class (think *Dead Poets Society*).

Dealing with problem spaces

Teachers often have to deal with a 'problem space' – one that is so difficult to work in that it affects the behaviour of their students. You might teach in an old, rundown school where the paint is peeling off the classroom walls. You could have to cope with a gym that is split into two for PE lessons, where only a flimsy partition separates you from the other class. Your room might have a huge bank of windows on one wall, making it freezing cold over the winter and boiling hot in the summer months.

My first ever classroom was the classic 'problem space'. The room was tiny, and I had some large Year 11 classes who would fill the space to bursting point. There were doors at either end of the classroom, and because the room linked two areas of the school together, it was seen as a useful corridor. The room was so long and narrow that some of the students had difficulty seeing the board. There was no room for movement once the classroom was full. The room would become progressively hotter as lessons wore on, particularly on summer afternoons when the sun shone straight into the room through windows without any blinds.

At the opposite extreme, I have also taught in a large, open drama space that caused me problems. This room had terrible acoustics because of a very high ceiling, and this meant that any noise the students made was amplified tenfold. Because the room was so large, the students' movement was completely unrestricted, and this led to behaviour problems as they ran around the space. There were also two levels in the room, with a 'stage' area from which the students could jump.

Unfortunately, it is a sad fact that many of us are 'stuck' with our problem rooms, for a whole school year or for even longer. Often the best we can do is find ways of minimizing the problems, so that our students are as comfortable and as well behaved as possible, and so that we feel relaxed too. Here are some thoughts and suggestions that you might find helpful.

Dealing with noise

Think about how you can reduce the overall noise level of your lessons. Keep your teaching voice low and controlled, encouraging your students to stay quiet to hear you. Use a silence command to gain whole-class attention, but choose one that involves minimal noise, such as raising your hand. Encourage the students to manage their own noise levels. For instance, when you want to use discussion activities, design a 'noise-o-meter' with the class, so that you can warn them when noise levels are getting too high.

To minimize your stress, you could divide your lessons into 'noisy' and 'quiet' times. For instance, follow a period of group work with a time for quiet reflection, perhaps watching groups of students present their ideas to the whole class, with the rest listening in silence. You might also take 'timeouts' from noise, when the class must work in complete silence for five minutes or so, to give you all a break.

Dealing with temperature

There are specified minimum and maximum temperatures for classrooms, and if you think that your own space might be contravening these rules, do get hold of a thermometer and check. Teachers sometimes suffer in silence, but health and safety regulations are designed to ensure staff/student comfort and safety. Talk to your union representative or manager about dealing with the problem of an excessively hot or cold room.

If sunlight heats up your classroom, then insist that blinds be fitted to your windows. In a hot space, students (and teachers) become ratty and bad-tempered more easily. Be aware of how the heat is affecting your temper, and try to stay calm and relaxed. Make sure that you dress appropriately for your room, and tell your students to do the same. If your school has a rule about students taking their coats off, but your classroom is freezing, this could lead to confrontations. Discuss the problem with a senior member of staff – could the rule be relaxed if the room falls below a certain temperature level?

Dealing with lack of space

Look at the way your classroom is laid out and experiment with different options, preferably before your students arrive at the beginning of the school year. Try putting your desks in groups rather than in rows, as this will generally take up less space. Think laterally too – perhaps it might help to turn the whole arrangement around, so that the desks are facing in an entirely different direction. If you have to store resources in a small space, ask for shelves to be put high up on the wall, so they don't take up any floor space. Chuck out any clutter that does not absolutely have to be in the room. Find ways to take your students out of the space to work on a fairly regular basis, for instance to the playground, hall, library or computer room.

The school environment and behaviour

There is a wide range of reasons for student misbehaviour, some of them totally unrelated to the skill of the individual teacher. Schools offer a very specific type of environment: one that can either encourage good behaviour or lead students to see poor behaviour as acceptable. If you work in a school with a strong and positive ethos, you may not be aware of all the factors that are contributing to good behaviour in your classroom. If you work in a school where behaviour tends to be an issue, you might be blaming yourself and your teaching, while external factors are at least partly to blame.

If you can develop an awareness of all the factors governing your students' behaviour, you are less likely to find yourself becoming stressed and defensive when they do misbehave. You can also take steps both to minimize any negative effects and also to change your own school situation for the better.

The school buildings

Our surroundings can have a strong impact on the way that we feel and behave. If the school you work in is rundown and dilapidated, with poor facilities, this could be having a negative effect on your students' behaviour. Their surroundings might make them feel low and depressed, as though the school does not really care about them. If the school population feels that no one cares about the buildings, this can lead to an increased incidence of vandalism and a general lack of care for the communal areas.

If you are in this situation, try to counteract it by making your classroom a sanctuary for your children. Put up colourful and interesting displays, so that as soon as your students walk through your classroom door, they are put into a more positive frame of mind. In addition, why not organize a group or a class of students to help brighten up one area of the school? If you are a PE teacher, you might like to arrange a team of painters to add a mural to the changing rooms. If you are a science specialist, you could organize a group of children to take responsibility for creating and maintaining a nature area.

169

The whole-school ethos

The school 'ethos' is quite a difficult concept to define. It basically refers to the prevailing culture, the way that the students perceive the school, and their behaviour and work within it. If the ethos of your school is a positive one, this will have far-ranging implications for behaviour in your own classroom. If students arrive at the school and find an ethos of hard work and good behaviour, it is likely (unless they have severe or specific individual problems) that they too will work hard and behave well.

Unfortunately, once the ethos of a school becomes negative, it can take years of work to put things right. The culture of poor discipline filters down through all ages of students, so that the behaviour of those at the top of the school creates a climate of challenging authority right the way through. This in turn can become a self-perpetuating cycle that is very hard to break.

There are some steps that you can take to help change the ethos of a school. Again, if you can turn your own classroom into a place where the negative ethos cannot penetrate, you will be contributing in a small but crucial way to the slow process of change. Teachers in a school with a negative ethos might tend to become cynical and demotivated, just like their students. Try to maintain a positive outlook, no matter how hard it is. If there are not many extra-curricular activities taking place in your school, you might organize a club to show your students how much you care about them, and about the school's progress as a whole.

Continuity of staff

'Good' schools find it relatively easy to attract and retain excellent teachers. The working conditions are good, the students want to learn, and the teachers enjoy their jobs so much that they don't actually want to leave. Unfortunately, for 'bad' schools, this situation is reversed. It is hard for these schools to recruit and retain well-motivated teachers, and the constant turnover of staff leads to a negative attitude in the students. The children start to feel that their teachers don't really care for them because they keep leaving. There is a lack of continuity in the teaching, especially if staff go midway through the school year. It is very hard for the teachers and students to develop positive relationships with each other, and staff can soon lose their motivation. With a high staff turnover, the school might find it hard to retain more experienced teachers, so that there is no one to mentor and help new recruits to the profession. This lack of continuity becomes a self-perpetuating downward spiral and it is hard for a school to break out of it.

Realistically, the best way for you to contribute to the continuity of staff within your own school is by staying there for a long time. In addition, you could support and mentor newer teachers, encouraging them to see the long-term picture, and creating a positive attitude amongst the staff. Obviously, it is up to you to decide whether you are willing to put up with the conditions in which you find yourself.

The management of the school

The way that a school is managed will have a significant impact on the behaviour that you experience within your classroom. The ideal is for the students to see a strong leadership team, who focus keenly on supporting and developing the staff of the school. There should be a sense that managers value their teaching staff highly, and are willing to back and support them in their work within the classroom. You should also feel that you can turn to your managers if you are having problems, and this will give you an added sense of security.

The management of a school is generally divided into a senior leadership team, including the headteacher, and one or more deputy or assistant heads. Below this is the curriculum management team, perhaps key stage or core subject leaders in a primary school, or heads of department or faculty in a secondary school. A supportive manager or head of department can be a huge bonus to a teacher who is struggling with control in his or her classroom. Your students should see a clear link between the normal teachers and the managers at your school. When the circumstances demand, teachers should be able to refer their most difficult students to a 'higher power' who can take the problem one stage further.

Whole-school behaviour policies

If it is effective and well thought out, your whole-school behaviour policy will be an invaluable aid in helping you control behaviour in your classroom. Different types of school have very different and specific behavioural problems, and ideally the whole-school behaviour policy should be linked closely to the particular difficulties your school faces. A good whole-school behaviour policy will offer teachers lots of motivational rewards, a number of sanction levels to work with when disciplining their students, and also a way of 'keeping tabs' on the overall behaviour of each individual within the school. Here are some of the factors that help make a whole-school behaviour policy effective.

- *It is created in conjunction with all the staff:* Teachers and other classroom staff have a very clear idea of what's going wrong (or right!) on a whole-school basis. They will often chat about behaviour problems in the staffroom, and in my experience tend to raise very similar concerns over whole-school behaviour issues. An effective management team will listen carefully to what their teachers say. They will develop their whole-school behaviour policy in conjunction with all staff, including the non-teaching members of the school. The staff will consequently feel a sense of ownership, and are far more likely to apply the policy consistently.
- *It undergoes a continuous process of change:* A good whole-school behaviour policy will be in a constant state of change. The policy needs to keep developing, not only to improve, but also because the staff and children are constantly changing as well.
- *It must be consistently applied:* Consistency is vital, so that the students know exactly what to expect from any teacher if they misbehave. There should be clear rules, and a clear pattern of sanctions that follow if students choose to break them.

Consistency is hard to achieve, because teachers are individuals who will apply the policy in their own different ways. However, where the policy is realistic, and agreed with all staff, it is much more likely to be consistently applied.

Below is a description of a typical whole-school behaviour policy, to show you how and why it might be effective. If you feel that your school behaviour policy is not working particularly well, you might like to suggest including some of the following ideas to help improve it. You will usually have the opportunity to do this through the meetings structure in your school.

The 'school rules'

The staff of the school need to decide exactly what types of behaviour are acceptable and unacceptable, creating a series of boundaries within which the teacher can work. This will probably result in a list of rules, whereby the students (and their parents) know exactly what is expected of them. These rules might refer to how they should work, to behaviour in the classroom and around the school building, and may also include details about uniform, and how the students should treat each other, their teachers, and the environment as a whole. It is useful for teachers to have a laminated set of these rules on the classroom wall, to refer to as you sanction. To be effective, school rules need to be short, clear and realistic. They should be phrased in a positive ('do this') rather than a negative ('don't do this') way.

A good set of rules will make the teacher's life easier. Teachers can refer to them when giving sanctions, making it clear that they are simply following the school policy, rather than personally 'attacking' the student. Some schools make life difficult for their staff by setting rules that will inevitably lead to confrontations. Some of the rules that teachers are asked to apply can seem remarkably petty, both to the teacher and to the students. When a teacher is put in this situation, it is clearly up to the individual how keenly they apply that particular rule. Unfortunately, once we start picking and choosing which rules we employ, the consistency of the whole-school behaviour policy is damaged. It is far better, surely, for schools to ensure that their rules are sensible in the first place, by consulting closely with their staff (and with their students).

Sanctions

Most schools operate a system of sanctions where the punishments build up gradually within a standardized format. The initial sanction might be a verbal warning, followed by a written warning, and then building up to detentions of increasing length. There might also be an added punishment for students who get to the highest level of sanction, for instance the teacher making a phone call home, or the child being sent out of the lesson.

A staged build-up of sanctions offers the teacher a good way of maintaining control, because there is a set pattern to follow in every instance. The steady build-up helps avoid confrontations, because there are plenty of chances for the student to decide to cooperate. Again, it is important that these levels are used consistently across the school, or the students may view certain teachers as unfair.

The 'ultimate' sanction

Most schools now have an 'ultimate' sanction, whereby a situation that has gone out of control can be retrieved, usually by removing the student from the classroom. It could be that a child is becoming physically violent, or simply that the teacher cannot continue the lesson if the student remains in the room. There should normally be a senior teacher available to come to the classroom and remove the student. The class teacher typically sends for help by using a 'red card' or a special slip. This is taken by a reliable student to the office to summon a senior teacher. Unfortunately, it is sometimes the case that teachers send for help and no one turns up, thus undermining the teacher and the power of the sanction.

It is perhaps a sad reflection of the situation in some of our classrooms that such a severe sanction could be necessary. The ultimate sanction should offer a 'fallback' position for when behaviour becomes completely unacceptable or even dangerous to the teacher and to the rest of the class. It should not be used as a way of repeatedly removing tricky students from the classroom. For this sanction to work properly, the teacher must not feel scared about using it, but must use it only when it is really necessary.

The points system

Much of the misbehaviour that teachers face on a daily basis is, thankfully, small-scale disruption rather than more serious incidents. However, these small-scale incidents can hamper learning if they are not dealt with effectively. Low-level interruptions are also a large cause of stress for teachers, because of their repetitive and irritating nature. There are many students who repeat a certain type of low-level misdemeanour over and over again. An effective school behaviour policy needs to have a way of monitoring and dealing with this problem.

One idea that I have seen used is a 'points system'. For each type of misdemeanour, the student earns (or loses) a certain number of points, ranging from one or two points for a small disruption or infraction, to a higher number of points for serious incidents. Points can also be given (or taken away) for breaking the school rules, for instance if a student is not in correct school uniform, or is late to school. The total level of points that a student has earned then allows the school to see exactly who is refusing to comply with the school code. This early warning system allows the teacher and the school to make an intervention at the appropriate time.

In-school behaviour units

Some schools (mainly secondary) now provide a specialist unit on site to which children with severe behavioural problems can be referred. Referrals might be part of a system of sanctions; for instance when a student reaches a certain level of points (see above) this could result in time spent in the behaviour unit.

175

These units are staffed by teachers experienced in dealing with behavioural issues. The unit should have a low teacher to student ratio, so that individual attention can be given to each child's needs, with the eventual aim of reintegrating the student back into the classroom.

Support systems

When we are having problems controlling behaviour, what we most need are good support systems, someone that we trust enough to share our worries with, or someone who can give us specialist advice on a particular issue. By its very nature, teaching is normally a solitary occupation, and working in your classroom you have very little idea about what is going on elsewhere in the school. It is all too easy for the imagination to run riot, and to find yourself thinking that all the other teachers in your school have perfect behaviour in *their* classrooms: to imagine that it is only you who *cannot* get the buggers to behave. Poor behaviour can make you feel depressed and alone, but with an effective support system in place, you will always have someone to turn to when you are feeling down.

Other teachers

Teachers tend to develop strong bonds with their colleagues, perhaps because the work that they do can be so physically and emotionally taxing. Although you probably spend little time during the day with other teachers, you may find yourself working alongside them during extra-curricular activities, or socializing with them outside of school. Try to find time to go to the staffroom during the day. This will give you a chance to refresh yourself – a tired teacher is far more likely to deal with poor behaviour in a negative way. It will also give you an opportunity to chat with other teachers about any problems you have experienced that day, to get some good tips and advice, or simply to let off steam.

Support staff

Increasingly, there are members of staff other than the teacher within the typical classroom. Although their key role is supporting learning, they will of course be invaluable to you in helping manage behaviour as well. Perhaps the best use of their time is in helping those children whose learning needs can lead to behaviour issues. For instance, if an individual child tends to mess around because he is struggling to understand the work, a teaching assistant could help him access the learning.

Special needs staff

The special needs staff at your school are an invaluable resource for you when dealing with behaviour in your classroom. Not only do they have specialist knowledge of the problems you are experiencing, they will also be aware of exactly how students' difficult behaviour can make you feel. Get to know these staff, ask their advice and get as much information from them as you can about how to handle your tricky children. Amongst these staff working with or at your school, there will typically be an SEN coordinator (SENCo), an educational psychologist (EdPsyc) and an educational welfare officer (EWO).

Managers

Your managers can also be a helpful source of comfort and inspiration. As with any staff in a school, though, the truth is that some managers will be effective and others will be less so. Teachers in a management position will have at least a few years' experience. If you are a relatively inexperienced teacher, they will be able to advise you because they will have already encountered many of the problems you are currently facing. Staff in management positions have a certain level of authority by virtue of their position in the hierarchy. Hopefully they can use this authority to help you manage behaviour, for instance by saying (in front of the class) that you can refer any particularly troublesome students to them.

Parents

Many parents are genuinely keen and willing to support the work that teachers do with their children, but often they have little idea of how to actually go about doing this. If an individual child is causing you problems because of his or her behaviour, take the time to contact the parents or guardians to discuss the situation. Often, parents are unaware of exactly what their children are doing at school. (After all, how many young people are going to confess their misbehaviour when they arrive home?) This is especially so in the secondary setting where there is relatively little contact between the school and the home. It could be that the parents are completely unaware of the problems that the child is creating, and that when you do advise them about what is going on, they are more than willing to back up the work that you are doing. The sense that your children's parents are supporting and helping you can give a real boost to the hard working-teacher.

The teaching unions

Your union representative can also be an excellent support, particularly if you are facing severe behaviour problems. There may be health and safety concerns involved (both with the room itself and with the students inside it), and your union representative can advise you about your legal position. If a student makes a complaint about you (an increasing problem nowadays, it seems) then your union representative will advise you on legal issues as well as other questions relating to your career.

13

Managing Behaviour in the Primary School

The primary school teacher and behaviour

Although the advice given in this book applies to students of all different ages, there are strategies which are best suited to controlling the behaviour of children at specific stages in their school life. This chapter gives you some tips and techniques aimed specifically at teachers working in the primary sector. There is advice about how to start out with a new class of young children, as well as ideas for developing your classroom control and helping in the transition to secondary school.

Young children can find school a confusing and frightening place, and we should take this into account when dealing with poor behaviour. At this stage, the pattern for the rest of the child's school career is being set, and clearly we want to create a positive model of good behaviour. Ideally, we need to avoid scaring young children into behaving well, and rather try to encourage them by using more positive means.

For children from a background of poor parenting skills, the primary school teacher may be the first adult to model appropriate behaviour. Just as a child who has not had much experience of books may prove to be a slow starter with literacy work, so a child who has never been taught what good behaviour is may take some time to settle into suitable patterns of behaviour for the school environment. A key part of the primary teacher's role is helping children develop an understanding of appropriate behaviour.

Starting out

The first few days and weeks with your class are crucial in setting the pattern for the entire year. This applies just as much to organizing good behaviour patterns as it does to encouraging proper work habits. For the primary school teacher, who works with a single class for the entire year, it is of course vitally important to create and develop good relationships with each individual child right from the start. Below are some useful tips and hints about starting out with a new class.

Gathering knowledge

It is tempting to spend a lot of time before the school year starts doing detailed planning, and ensuring that your lessons are organized well in advance. However, until you have actually met and got to know the children with whom you will be working, some of this time might actually be better spent on gathering knowledge about the class. That way, when you do come to plan, you will have a much better chance of differentiating appropriately, and suiting the work to your children's needs and interests. There is a range of ways in which you can gather information:

- *Talk to your colleagues:* Unless you are working with a nursery or Reception class, many of your children will have been taught in previous years by other members of staff at your school. If possible, take some time to discuss the class with your colleagues before the children arrive. Avoid making judgements about what to expect based only on another teacher's impressions. However, your colleagues may be able to give you some useful tips about specific behavioural issues or particular mixes of children.
- *Consider special needs:* Spend time talking to any special needs staff who work in or consult with your school. Find out about any children who have specific learning or behavioural difficulties, or physical difficulties. Get hold of any reports, individual education plans or other written material about your children. Read this through to get an overview of what to expect.
- *Learn the names:* The quicker you learn your children's names, the better you will be able to control their behaviour. Here are some ideas about how to do this:
  - Make a display with a picture of each child and his or her name alongside. The children could add information about their interests, hobbies, etc.
  - Play some name games on the first few days. These are a useful warm-up exercise, and will also help the children get to know each other.

- When the children are at desks, use a seating plan, to help you learn names and demonstrate control. Use the reward of free seating choice as a useful carrot for good behaviour.
- *Get to know the children:* Rather than plunging straight into the curriculum, take time to get to know your children as individuals. You might talk about 'my favourite things' at circle time, or split the class into groups to share their personal talents or interests.

Teaching classroom behaviour

In the early years of the primary school, the children will not have had much or any experience of classrooms. In fact, even children higher up the primary school, and indeed in secondary school, often find it difficult to maintain behaviours such as sitting still, raising a hand to answer a question, concentrating on their work, and so on. These skills and behaviours can be taught, and the primary school is the best place for this learning to take place, particularly at the start of the school year. Some of the classroom behaviours which you might teach include:

- *Sitting behaviour:* Teach the children how to sit properly on the carpet and on a chair. For instance, crossing their legs, folding their arms and 'keeping themselves to themselves' when sitting on the carpet. Explain the importance of not 'tipping back' on chairs, and of staying seated unless the teacher gives permission to get up.
- *Listening behaviour:* You want your children to be silent and attentive when you talk. By far the best time to teach good listening behaviour is right at the start of the year. Use lots of eye contact to check for their attention. Encourage the children to fold their arms to help them avoid fidgeting.
- *Answering behaviour:* Teach your children the correct process for answering a question: hands up, don't call out, everyone tries to participate, etc. Use prompts to ingrain the right habits, for example asking 'Put up your hand if you can tell me. . .'.
- *Working behaviour*: Be clear with your children about exactly how they should approach their work. You might go through

a set of work habits and even put a list of these up on the wall, for the class to follow. For instance, with Year 5 or 6 children, your list might include:
- Always put a title and date, and underline it.
- Write as neatly as you can.
- Take time to check your work for spelling and punctuation.
- Work in silence (or only talk quietly during work time).
- Put your hand up if you have a question or if you need help.

'Training' your children

In the film *Kindergarten Cop*, Arnold Schwarzenegger trains his class of young children as though they were at a 'police academy'. This fictional example demonstrates a very effective point about working with young children. If you can train them to behave well right at the beginning, they will (usually) happily follow your instructions from then onwards. Effectively, this 'training' involves explaining your expectations and demonstrating them to the class. You might train your children in:

- *The morning routine:* What should the children do on arriving at the classroom first thing in the morning? Do they get their books and equipment ready on the desks? Do they sit silently in their seats or on the carpet so that the teacher can take the register? Should they line up outside the room until the teacher allows them inside?
- *Responses to teacher signals:* Ideally, you want the class responding quickly and routinely to your control signals, so that it is easy to gain the children's attention. Their responses will eventually become a matter of habit, and this will mean far less effort need be expended on your part.
- *Dealing with equipment:* Train your children in collecting and using equipment. In the long run this will save you time and effort, and it will also encourage your students to take responsibility for their own behaviour and learning. For instance, you might have a set of drawers where your children keep their things. On a signal from you, they could be trained to go to the drawers a few at a time, collect their equipment

and return to their seats. You can spice this up by turning it into a game or competition for the 'best' team.

- *Tidying up the classroom:* Similarly, train your children in putting resources and equipment away and in tidying up the classroom at the end of each lesson or each day. You might nominate a 'team' with responsibility for ensuring that each area of the room is clean and organized.

Techniques for classroom control

Keeping control of your children in a calm and consistent way is one of the key factors in maintaining good behaviour. There will always be some individual students who make life difficult for you through their behaviour, but generally speaking it is the low-level disruptions which cause the teacher the most stress, and these often result from a class that is not fully under control. The tips below cover a number of aspects in your day-to-day classroom management. Many of these good habits can be introduced during those vital first few weeks.

Getting your children's attention

In the primary school, and especially with very young children, finding an effective way to get the class's attention is important for good classroom control. You may find that your students have become totally engrossed in their work, or that they are involved in a noisy activity. Obviously, you want to avoid shouting when you need them to listen. Instead, you must find a way to gain their attention quickly and easily, while maintaining a calm and positive atmosphere. This is where control signals can come in very handy. Here are a number of different ideas for gaining your children's attention – these can easily be developed into habits with your class.

- *The non-verbal signal:* The teacher agrees a specific signal to indicate 'I want your attention' with the class, and the children must look out for this. For instance, the use of a 'silent seat', whereby the teacher sits in a particular chair and this is a signal that the class must come straight to the carpet. Another example is the teacher raising a hand to indicate that all the children should stop what they are doing, fall silent, and raise their hands too.

- *The time target:* This is a useful technique because it places the responsibility on the children, rather than the teacher, for controlling behaviour. Before starting an activity, the teacher sets the class a challenge: they must keep an eye on the clock, and at a time specified by the teacher they should fall silent in preparation for the next instruction. At the appointed time you will usually find one or two more observant individuals 'shushing' the rest of the class for you.
- *The targeted command:* For this control signal, the teacher calls out a quick, targeted signal, such as '3, 2, 1, freeze!' On 'freeze', the class must freeze as still as statues. By making this command into a 'game', you can challenge your children to respond more quickly each time the game is played.
- *The sound signal:* The teacher plays a brief burst of music, or gives a quick whistle or other sharp sound, to indicate that it is time for the children to stop work and pay attention. Those students who stop fastest might be rewarded in some way, to encourage a quicker response each time.
- *'We all join in':* For me, this technique has proved perhaps one of the most effective methods of gaining attention, particularly with the younger end of the primary age range. The teacher starts clicking her fingers or clapping his hands in a pattern, for instance two slow clicks followed by three fast ones. The children must then join in with the pattern. Because they are concentrating on copying the teacher's rhythm, the children stop talking. The teacher then slows down the clicking or clapping gradually, until the class all stop at the same moment, ready to pay attention.

Keeping your children's attention

Young children are easily distracted. In fact, using distraction is a useful way of diverting your students from poor behaviour, for instance when a finger puppet suddenly appears to distract little Annie from her tantrum. However, this also means that the teacher must work hard to keep the attention of a class of young children, particularly during explanations of work and other teacher-led activities. You will also want to ensure that your children maintain their attention on work activities during the course of each lesson. The techniques described below will help you to achieve this.

- *Keep eye contact:* As you talk with your class, keep your eyes moving around to ensure that every child is looking right at you. If you notice a student who is not, pause for a moment, without saying anything. The child will usually pick up on the fact that you have stopped speaking, and look at you to find you staring straight at him or her.
- *Repeat back to me:* When you are explaining the work, it is easy for children to look as though they are listening when in fact the words are not actually registering in their minds. After you've finished a run-through of the lesson tasks, ask a student to repeat back what you have just said (preferably a child who you suspect was not really listening). In this way you can clarify any misunderstandings before the children begin work.
- *Break up your lessons:* Break up longer lessons into smaller task chunks, so that you can keep your children focused and reward them for completing each activity. When you offer breaks between tasks, use this opportunity for the children to 'stretch' themselves. This might be a brain stretch, such as some quick mental arithmetic, or a physical stretch, for instance everyone standing up to shake out their bodies.

Giving instructions

It can be hard for young children to take in all the things that are going on around them. After all, only recently their parents or guardians were their whole world. Now they are at school, where many different things are going on, and they can be easily sidetracked. This means that it is vital for the primary teacher to learn how to give effective instructions, for instance when explaining the work that must be done during the lesson. It is actually surprisingly hard to give clear instructions: it's a skill that comes with lots of practice.

If the children do not fully understand your instructions, all sorts of disruptions can arise. You set the class off to work, only to find that five hands immediately go up, with children saying 'I don't understand what I'm meant to do'. You then have to spend valuable lesson time explaining a task over again to individuals. Those children who are not confident enough to ask for help might turn to misbehaviour to cover up their lack of understanding. You can overcome all these issues by giving effective instructions in the first place. Here are some tips about how to do this.

- *Be as clear as possible:* Although the instructions you give might seem clear to you, often they will prove surprisingly confusing to your students. You have the lesson planned in your mind, but getting that lesson over to the children can be very tricky. To ensure clarity, overexaggerate the simplicity of your instructions, aiming them at the weakest, most confused child in the class. Speak with a slow and well-modulated voice, emphasizing any key words as you talk.
- *Back it up visually:* Some children will find it much easier to understand what they can see rather than what they can hear. Find lots of visual ways to reinforce your instructions – drawing diagrams on the board, writing up key points on the board, using props, and so on.
- *Give an example:* Going through examples with the class will really reinforce what you want them to do. An example helps us take an idea from the abstract concept to the concrete activity. Where possible, ask for volunteers to help you go through these examples, to encourage participation and help you check for understanding.
- *Consider your vocabulary:* As adults, we use words without really considering the need for understanding. For young children, with a limited vocabulary, care is needed to ensure that every word is easily understood. Be as specific as you can

187

– instead of saying 'take care with your punctuation', ask your children to ensure that they 'put all the full stops and commas in the right places'.

- *Use time indicators:* To avoid a jumble of instructions, make the order and timing of the work very clear. For instance, to clarify the order, tell your children that 'first I want you to do ...'. Set time limits or targets for each task to indicate how long the children have to complete the work, perhaps writing these on the board for reference.

- *The 'rule of three':* Children seem to find it hard to retain more than about three instructions at once – this appears to be the maximum amount of information that they can process at any one time. When giving instructions, limit yourself to the three main points which the children must retain.

- *Use lots of repetition:* Train yourself to repeat instructions over and over again, in a range of ways, to ensure you have complete understanding. Ask for students to repeat back what you have said to them, to check for any areas of weak comprehension.

- *Get help from teaching assistants and other staff:* Share information about activities with any support staff, preferably before the lesson. They can then assist you in giving explanations to any children who don't understand.

Make behaving well fun

There are many ways that you can 'trick' your children into behaving well without them realizing that this is your intention. If you make behaving well seem like fun, this will create a positive atmosphere in your classroom. It will also put a lot less stress on you as a teacher over the course of the school year. Here are some ideas about how to do this:

- *Turn control tasks into a 'game':* Think about the way that you present tasks and activities to your children. Use language that suggests fun and challenge rather than boredom and hard work. For instance, you might want your Reception class to lie down and be still for story time at the end of the school day.

Instead of telling the children the required behaviour in a dull way, introduce the task as a game called 'sleeping lions', in which they must pretend to be lions who are fast asleep.

- *Enter the world of make-believe:* Children of all ages respond to make-believe and to the chance to use their imaginations – the opportunity to be someone, something or somewhere they are not. For example, if you want the class to tidy up the room very quietly, you might tell them to imagine that beneath the floor is a sleeping giant, and that they are walking across his back and must not wake him.

- *Treat them as adults:* One very useful fiction for the primary school teacher is that of the children gradually becoming more adult and grown up. For instance, you might ask your class to play the role of science professors while working on an experiment. Taking on the role of an expert in this way encourages the children to take responsibility for their work and behaviour. Interact with them as though they are adults, expressing surprise at any silliness: 'I can hardly believe you're doing that, Professor Smith, seeing as you're a world-renowned scientist.'

Towards the secondary school

By the time they reach Year 6 in the primary school, students are preparing to make the transition from child to young adult. They are on the cusp of becoming teenagers, but are not yet quite ready to shrug off some of the childish feelings and emotions which may lead to immature and silly behaviour. In the top year of primary or middle education, your students may have an added sense of confidence as a result of being the 'top dogs' in the school. Things change dramatically when they arrive at secondary school, where they are once again at the bottom of the pile.

At this age, some students may start to push at the boundaries and test out adult authority, as they take the first steps on the road to becoming a grown-up. Consequently, you will need to adapt the strategies you use to suit the age of the children you teach. Here are a few ideas for working with those students at the top of the primary school:

- *Take them seriously:* At this age, children often view themselves as more grown up than they actually are. If you want them to behave in a mature fashion, then take their feelings seriously. Never talk down to them. If you patronize them, they will react badly; if you treat them as young adults, they will often live up to your expectations. Children this age may surprise you with the adult way in which they are able to act and behave.
- *Offer a positive role model:* Positive role models can become particularly important at this age, as children move beyond the desire to simply ape their parents, and start learning from external influences. The teacher can have a very positive influence on the students; similarly, other students can also offer constructive or harmful examples. If you teach a Year 6 class, they will probably be nervous and uncertain about the transition to secondary school. You might invite a secondary school student in to offer them a positive example and to talk to them about what the move will entail.
- *Know what interests them:* This is a time when children start to take a keen interest in the wider world, and the cultural icons surrounding them in the media. They are starting to gain their independence, and their parents may be giving them more freedom to buy their own clothes and music, or to stay out later in the evenings. Find out what interests your class – the latest boy band, or the popular football player – and try to incorporate these interests into your teaching. At the very least you can chat to your students to show that you are up to date on the latest cultural developments. Personalizing your teaching in this way will help you encourage better behaviour.
- *Understand their fears and concerns:* At this age children become more sensitive to peer group pressures. They may be fearful of being left out of the group, and they may start to feel embarrassed about their relationships with the opposite gender. Think back to how you felt at this age – and if you

ask your students to work in boy/girl pairs, do not be surprised
if they react negatively.

Handling the transition

The transition from primary or middle to secondary school can be
an extremely difficult time for our students. In Year 6, they will
be full of concerns about what secondary school might actually
be like; once they reach Year 7, they may find the new
environment confusing and threatening. If we can minimize
the trauma that the transition causes, then we can hopefully also
reduce the negative effects on behaviour that may result. Here
are some suggestions to help:

- *Organize visits:* Many schools (both primary and secondary)
  now have a teacher whose responsibility it is to oversee the
  transition to secondary school. This teacher might help
  organize visits to the secondary school for students in Year
  6, and hold sessions in which any questions can be answered.
- *Discuss the differences:* The class teacher can help by discussing
  the differences between primary and secondary school with
  the class. For instance, the fact that they will have different
  teachers for different subjects, moving around the school
  rather than staying in one place for the majority of the time.
- *Help them get organized:* Talk to your class about how they
  might best organize themselves – they can do this over the
  summer before they start at secondary school. For example,
  ensuring that they have the right equipment, packing their
  bags the night before school, getting uniform out and ready to
  put on in the mornings.
- *Pen pals:* Another useful idea is for Year 6 students to make
  pen pals with their Year 7 counterparts in local schools. By
  exchanging letters, they can find out from the older students
  the 'truth' about secondary school. Hopefully this will help
  dispel many of those rumours which amazingly still float
  around, such as having your head flushed down the toilet.
  Having a 'contact' at secondary school can also lessen the fear

when they do start at the new school – at least the Year 6
students will know one person when they arrive.
- *Mentors:* Similarly, some schools now offer older mentors to
  pair up with the primary students in their first year of
  secondary school. These mentors typically come from Year 9/
  10 or above. Again, it is useful for young students to have a
  contact – someone to help them settle in.

14

Managing behaviour in the secondary school

The secondary school teacher and behaviour

Just as in the primary school, there are certain techniques that will work particularly well when dealing with older students. You can find lots of ideas for secondary-specific strategies in this chapter. The secondary teacher often has to deal with a whole range of age groups in a single day – children, teenagers, young adults. Adapting your style to fit each of these age groups is an important and subtle skill for the secondary school specialist.

The top end of secondary can be a very rewarding age group to teach in terms of subject delivery – you get to teach your subject at a level that stretches and challenges you. However, it can also be one of the most challenging situations when behaviour is a problem. A number of your students may be physically larger than you, and if they are confrontational, the teacher can be made to feel threatened and vulnerable. By this age disaffection with education can cause problems in motivation, particularly in some subject areas.

Students at GCSE, AS and A level are practically grown up, and in our modern world they have many adult concerns that are nothing to do with education. There is also a great deal of pressure on students in the lead-up to exams. Some of your students will be ready to leave education, moving out of the safe, enclosed school environment and into the real world.

Starting out

The first few lessons with any class are vital in setting the scene for a good year. For the secondary teacher, the beginning of term means meeting and getting to know large numbers of young people, and this can prove very stressful indeed. Learning names is a real issue, especially for the teacher of a 'once a week' subject such as music, art, PE or drama, who may be teaching hundreds of different children. Below you can find some ideas for dealing with those critical first few weeks of term and setting yourself up for success.

A question of style

Striking the right note with your classes is something that worries many teachers, and particularly those who are just starting out in the profession. Unless you can define your style early on, and stick to the same approach each time you see the class, your students will quickly identify weakness, uncertainty and inconsistency. The thoughts given on style below are based very much on my own favoured approach and what I have found works best. Bear in mind that you will need to adapt all the advice I give to your own school and the kind of students that you teach.

I would advise all secondary teachers to start the year with a fairly hard, strict style – to be as strict as you feel you can get away with. I don't necessarily agree with the old adage 'Don't smile at them until Christmas', but I certainly believe that you put yourself in a much stronger position if you start out tough. Funnily enough, this applies perhaps even more if you are working at what you consider an easy school, where you may be lulled into a false sense of security during the 'honeymoon period' with your classes. A tough approach means that the students are given a very clear and assertive impression of you as a teacher. There is no uncertainty; no space for them to try it on. I have also found that students actually prefer, and respect, a teacher who works in this way early on. There is no room for messing about – the work takes priority, and they seem to respond to this.

In some very tough schools, you might need to take care with an overly strict or assertive style. Where the teacher's style is interpreted as aggression rather than assertion, this can cause students to react badly. With some particularly difficult children, you may need to take a more laid-back and relaxed style, coaxing them onto your side rather than demanding that they comply. On the whole, though, children do like their teachers to be figures of authority (although not authoritarian). You can adapt your style according to the age of the students – generally speaking, with Year 7 you can play it very strict, gradually relaxing as you move up the years.

Once the students are fully under control, you can make a gradual relaxation in your style, providing you with a useful carrot/reward factor. Do not, however, relax too soon or too quickly, particularly in your first few years of teaching. I would recommend the first half-term as being a suitable length of time for a tough style to be communicated, and then a 'drip feed' of slightly more flexibility being applied. Being hard and tough definitely does not mean being rude, or being negative; it simply means being extremely certain and definite about what will go on in your lessons, staying calm no matter what the provocation. Some of the ways in which a 'tough' style might be communicated include:

- Making the students line up outside the room, single file, facing front, in silence, before they are allowed inside.
- Taking the register, in total silence, at the beginning of each lesson. In addition to the silence, ensuring that your students are sitting still throughout. (Don't try this one unless you are pretty sure that you are going to achieve it.)
- Insisting that written work be done in complete silence. This can be offset by the 'generous gift' of two-minute timeouts to talk.
- Adhering like glue to any uniform rules, such as coats off, no trainers, blazers on, ties done up in a certain way.
- Stamping down on small breaches of the rules, for instance the chewing of gum.

It's the small things that count

Carrying on from the point above, when you are trying to stamp your authority on a class at the start of the year, it really is the small things that count. I've found this strategy particularly useful when I work as a supply teacher. In fact it's helpful in any situation where you're covering someone else's lessons and you are at the mercy of any poorly behaved students. Use the first few minutes of the lesson to pick up on any minor rule-breaking immediately, to show how definite and aware you are. Some of the 'small things' on which I might pick up would include:

- coats off;
- shirts tucked in;
- ties done up properly;
- no chewing;
- sitting properly in chairs;
- correct equipment out;
- looking at me while I'm talking.

Setting up the patterns

As well as demonstrating your control, the first few lessons of the year are a time when you can set up the patterns of how your class will run. These patterns are especially vital in the secondary school, because the students you teach will be experiencing a variety of approaches from all their different teachers. If you can provide a well-structured, clear and consistent pattern to your lessons, you can 'train' them to keep to these work and behaviour habits each time you see them. The more consistent you can be, the more secure your children will feel (especially those who tend towards poor behaviour). You can see an example of a teacher setting up the lesson pattern in Chapter 2. Some of the questions you will need to consider about your own pattern are:

- What do the students do when they first arrive at your classroom?
- Are they allowed to come straight in, or required to fulfil certain criteria first (such as lining up in silence)?
- Where is the teacher when the class arrives at the lesson?
- What happens when the students enter the room?
- How do the students know where to sit? Is this a free choice or not?
- At what point, and how, are equipment and resources put on the desks?
- At what stage in the lesson is the register taken?
- How must the students behave during the taking of the register?
- How does the teacher go about explaining the work that will be done?

- How must the students behave while this explanation takes place?
- In what atmosphere does work take place (i.e. total silence or not)?
- What happens at the end of the lesson? How is the work reviewed?
- Do the students have to stand behind their chairs?
- At what point is homework set?
- How does the teacher dismiss the class?

Techniques for classroom control

When working with secondary-aged students, the techniques you use can generally be a little harder or closer to the edge than those you might use with younger children. Of course, how far you can go will depend a great deal on what your own individual school finds acceptable. One of the skills of the teacher is understanding and demonstrating where the boundaries are, but at the same time showing your students that you are not afraid to push at these boundaries where it means you can achieve better results from and for your classes. If you are working with students who genuinely like and respect you, you can afford to show your humanity by stretching the limits yourself once in a while.

Getting them silent

As you've probably realized by now, it's my feeling that waiting for silence is one of the most important and powerful control techniques that a teacher can use. For some (perhaps many) secondary teachers, this can be a very difficult aim to actually achieve with some classes. Of course, I too have stood at the front of a class, waiting for silence and feeling certain that I will never fulfil my aim. I am fully aware of how nerve-racking it can be to keep on waiting, and how tempting it is to give in and just start talking over those students who do refuse to be quiet.

However, it really is crucial to consider the signals you are sending to the class every time you do give up on this particular expectation. Basically, your action is telling them that you don't mind them talking while you are speaking, or that you simply don't believe you have enough control over them to achieve total silence. On the other hand, the teacher who does gain complete silence from the class before being willing to speak is sending a very powerful message about his or her level of control.

Waiting for silence is my number one expectation, and one that I am willing to fight for, no matter how long it takes. In one school, I fought with some classes for two whole terms over this expectation, but I never gave up on what I wanted to achieve. Of course, when I say 'wait' for silence, there are a number of different strategies that you can employ to encourage your students along the road to fulfilling your expectation. The more ideas you have under your belt, the less likely you are to give up on achieving that wonderful, silent and attentive class. Here are a few techniques particularly applicable to secondary school classes:

- *The written signal:* If you need to sanction your class to gain silence, try not to speak to them, as this lessens the impression of teacher status and control. Try instead writing their potential punishment on the board. This might be as simple as drawing a blank circle, then standing looking at your watch very deliberately for a minute, before drawing a number '1' in the circle. Gradually increase the number of minutes to be spent in detention after the lesson, until the students are silent. Alternatively, try writing a long sentence as your message to the class, for instance, 'If you won't all be silent and let me get on with teaching the lesson, then you will force me to keep you in at break time, and I really don't want to have to do that.' By the time you've finished writing that, hopefully the whole class will be looking to see what you're doing. Although I'm not a fan of whole-class detentions, I have generally found that after a couple of times of using these approaches, the students give up on talking over me and fall into line.
- *Use a 'minutes lesson':* There will be some classes that you teach where there is not a break immediately after the lesson. In

these circumstances, you can't use the threat of break time detentions to gain silence (unless you plan to try and get the whole class back to you at break time, and I'd strongly advise against it). The great idea of a 'minutes lesson' was given to me by a teacher as a way of solving this issue. Say you see a class three times a week – twice at a time when they do not have break after the lesson, but once at the end of the day or before a break or lunchtime. Simply designate this as your 'minutes lesson', then save up any minutes owed to you for talking to be served at this time.

- *The theatrical gesture:* If you have a bit of the drama queen or king in your soul, then you might like to use this unusual technique to achieve silence. Theatrical gestures are great for getting the class's attention, and usually raise a laugh. You might (pretend to) bang your head on your desk and start sobbing, saying to yourself, 'Why oh why won't they be silent? I just can't cope anymore. Oh what am I going to do!?' You could say, 'Right! That's it, I've had enough! I'm going to fetch the head!' and then pretend to storm out of the door.

- *Big Brother is watching you:* With my most difficult classes, I have resorted to using this technique to gain silence and attention, despite complaints from my children about how their civil rights were being infringed. To use the strategy, set up a video camera in the corner of the room, and then as soon as the class enter the room start recording. Tell your children that the headteacher will be watching the tape after the lesson to see which students are misbehaving and refusing to become silent. This might be a bluff, or you could actually arrange this beforehand with a sympathetic head. In my experience, the children are unwilling to take the risk that what you say might be true. Erase the tapes once the strategy has worked, to avoid any problems with video permissions.

Treat them as adults

Students will typically live up (or down) to what we expect of them. If you treat your secondary school students as adults you may well be surprised at the mature way in which they behave.

Of course, along with your adult treatment of your classes comes their responsibility for behaving and working in the appropriate manner. I like to make this 'partnership' between students and teacher very explicit to my classes from the first lesson. And if the students decide not to fulfil their end of the bargain, then I am perfectly entitled to withdraw any privileges they have been given.

To all intents and purposes, students at the top end of the secondary age range are effectively adults. If you want respect and good behaviour from them, you will need to talk to them and work with them on an adult level. There really is little point in being a 'strict and scary' teacher at this stage (although my advice about being tough still applies). These young adults will generally react badly to a confrontational style, and are sensitive to the feeling that they are being patronized. After all, in the real world, for instance at work, people would talk to them politely if there was a problem, rather than shouting at them. Why should things be any different at school?

I heard a very interesting idea recently, about outlining expectations for young adults or students at FE level. This was the teacher who, in his first lesson, came into the room and drew a line on the board. He asked the class: 'What's this?' Eventually the answer came: 'It's a line.' His reply: 'That's right. Make sure you don't step over it.'

Sometimes treat them as children

Paradoxically, older students will also respond very well to being given childish tasks or activities from time to time. The serious nature of much of the work at secondary school means it is important for them to have the chance to blow off steam on occasions, and to take part in some really fun, silly activities or lessons. This also shows your willingness to demonstrate a more human side. Here are a few ideas about how you might allow your secondary-aged students some childlike moments:

- *Games:* Students really respond well to the teacher who offers the chance to play a few games, perhaps at the start or end of

201

the lesson. These games could be subject related, or just a general activity to lighten the atmosphere. Some games are actually very educational: for instance I use an adaptation of the TV programme *Call my Bluff* during English lessons. If it makes you feel more comfortable, you might designate these games as your 'starter activity' or 'plenary'.

- *Quizzes:* An excellent way to end a topic is to offer your class a quiz, rather than a test, on the subject covered. Students generally like to work in groups, as this takes some of the pressure off the less able individuals. Making the quiz into a competitive event, with prizes at the end, will encourage greater effort and commitment.
- *Make a mess:* Once in a while, put your inhibitions aside and allow your students to do a fun, messy activity. This could be framed as a reward for recent good behaviour. One activity that secondary school students love is to be given piles of magazines and asked to cut out pictures to create a collage related to the subject. For instance, I have had classes creating characters in a drama lesson by sticking together various bits of different people's bodies. Just one tip – make sure you leave plenty of time for clearing up at the end of the lesson.

Use humour to sanction

If a student swears, either at you or just out loud, they expect to be told off. What they don't expect, however, is for you to ask them (in a disappointed, shocked, horrified or just deadpan voice) *'Do you know what the word ''****'' actually means?'* Surprisingly often, students don't actually know why the swear words they use are offensive or what their literal meaning is. This applies particularly to younger students, trying to ape their older counterparts. They may simply have heard these words used in the playground (or the classroom), and picked up on the effect that using them achieves.

If you ask this question in a deadly serious way, you will probably find the rest of the class start to laugh. They will be laughing partly at the student's (probable) embarrassment, but also at the sound of hearing a teacher use a swear word. By putting the word in verbal speech marks, and simply quoting what the student has said, you are of course not actually swearing. On a more serious note, by confronting the behaviour, and the problems with it, students are forced to consider why they should change. They are also made to realize the impact on other people that hearing these words can have.

Please note that whether or not you should use this technique depends a great deal on the kind of teacher you are, the school you work in, and the reactions you are likely to receive. If you feel that your children, their parents or your headteacher would not be comfortable with a teacher using this strategy, don't actually repeat the swear word that the child has used. Ask instead: 'Do you know what that word actually means?'

The form tutor and behaviour

Many secondary teachers will also be expected to take on a pastoral role within the school, registering a tutor or form group and taking responsibility for this group's overall progress and welfare at the school. Working with a form group is a very different prospect to working with a class in a specific subject area. In fact, you might not actually be timetabled to teach any of your form group at all.

How you handle the behaviour of your tutor group will depend on two main factors: the expectations of the school as to how form tutors should work, and also the age and type of students in your group. On the whole, you can afford to take a more relaxed approach to the role of form tutor. You can adapt the style that you use as a subject teacher, and consequently develop a different sort of relationship with these students. This more relaxed relationship is important, because your form tutees may be coming to you with personal or social concerns, and they need to feel free to talk openly. Here is some general advice about managing behaviour as a form tutor:

- *Match your approaches to the age group:* If you are given a class of first years, then you have a wonderful chance to 'train them up' in your ways of working. Again, I would advise you to start out with a fairly firm approach, which can be relaxed a little over time. On the other hand, if you are given a rowdy group in their last year of formal schooling, who have had four different tutors over the years, then there is little point in giving yourself a stressful time by trying to crack the whip too hard.

– *Keep a check on equipment:* With younger students, the tutor can help children to organize themselves properly, and consequently to avoid pointless sanctions for missing equipment, etc. With a first year group, you might do an equipment check with your students at the start of each day or week.

– *Keep an overview of sanctions and rewards:* Most schools now use diaries, in which teachers can record the sanctions and rewards earned. Tutors can take a helpful overview of how well (or badly) each student is doing, and if necessary provide an early alert system for more senior staff.

– *Sort out the issues that waste lesson time:* The tutor can act as a useful support and back-up for subject teachers, by sorting out those minor issues that can really eat into lesson time. For instance, ensure that your students have shoes on rather than trainers, before they head off for the day's lessons.

– *Consider how best to take the register:* With younger students, you will probably be able to insist on and get total silence for taking the register. With some older classes, such an approach will only set you up for confrontations. If you are likely to have difficulty getting the class silent, then ask for a volunteer to help you check who is and is not present. You should mark the register yourself, as it is a legal document and the tutor's responsibility.

– *Keep a teacher/tutor divide:* If you do teach members of your form group for lessons, then you will probably need to make it clear to them that the two roles are distinct. Have a quiet word with any individuals who push at the boundaries, clarifying the different roles that you play in class and tutor time.

GCSE and beyond

Although I advise teachers to start out tough with secondary school students, once you have gained their respect, attention, commitment and hard work, you can afford to apply a little flexibility. There should be very much a sense of partnership – your students earn the right to certain freedoms if they demonstrate a willingness to go along with what you ask in terms of work and behaviour. I have found that this flexibility is particularly appropriate and important when working with GCSE classes and above. Here are some tips as to how you can achieve and manage a more flexible approach with young adults:

- *Be willing to stretch the boundaries:* Some of the rules and boundaries that are set in a school can seem pretty meaningless to students at the higher end of the age range. After all, why shouldn't they wear a coat if they are cold, or chew gum if they wish? Your priority at this stage is their learning. After initially establishing control over the situation, you should avoid the rigid application of petty rules when appropriate, especially if these are likely to lead to friction. For instance, these young adults see swearing all around them – on the television, in their social life, from their families and friends. Ignoring the odd swear word will make you seem more human, and will also help you avoid pointless conflict with your classes.
- *Make them take responsibility:* Once out in the world, and working in a job, your students will need to behave properly, or they will be sacked. At this stage of their school lives, they must take responsibility for their behaviour and for their learning. Point this out to them when they do misbehave. If you treat them like adults, they must learn to take an adult level of responsibility for their behaviour. Expect the best from them and hopefully you won't be disappointed.
- *Understand their concerns:* At this age, your students may have some serious concerns that are unconnected to their schooling. They may be having boy or girlfriend problems that affect the way they behave in your lessons. Do try to understand this

205

– just as you have worries outside of school, so do they. If you are a particularly sympathetic teacher, you may find that some of your students approach you to talk about a personal problem. Do make sure that you take the time to discuss their problem on an adult level with them. Ensure too that you refer the difficulty to the relevant member of staff at your school if it seems necessary, particularly if it is a child welfare issue, such as a teenage pregnancy.

Part Five
FOR
EXAMPLE ...

15
'MINOR'
BEHAVIOUR
PROBLEMS

The examples

The next two chapters give examples of teachers dealing with various behaviour problems. By reading these examples you will get to see how the ideas in this book actually work in practice. The examples deal with various different incidents of misbehaviour and are set at a variety of ages across the primary and secondary sectors, although the approaches taken are applicable to any age group.

For each incident, I give two examples to show how a teacher might handle the problem in a 'good' or a 'bad' way. The examples are written as play scripts with some general information about the situation, then a chance to see how the teacher deals with the problem. At the end of each example I give a commentary, discussing what the teacher did, the strategies he or she used (or failed to use), and exactly how these tactics worked. Of course, it's inevitable that these play scripts will be a bit simplistic – it's hard to capture the complex realities of classroom life in written form. But my hope is that they will give you an overview of how the strategies described in this book might work in real life.

First I look at some 'minor' behaviour problems, low-level disruptions such as a talkative class or a student who is chewing gum. It is usually relatively easy to deal with these problems. Where the teacher is seen to solve minor difficulties in a calm and consistent way, this will encourage better behaviour from all the students. It will also help prevent more serious confrontations, because the students see that they cannot get away with anything, no matter how minor. On the other hand, if these problems are dealt with badly, situations can be exacerbated so that more serious incidents do occur. Just take a look at the 'bad' examples to see what can happen when things get out of hand.

The talkative class

Age group: Year 7.
Details of the problem: Although this class is generally good natured and well behaved, they can be incredibly talkative. This

208

is causing Miss Flynn problems, particularly at the start of the lesson when she wants to settle them down, take the register, and get on with the work.

A good example

The class arrive for their lesson, chatting away happily. Miss Flynn is standing at the door, blocking the entrance, arms folded, looking mean.

Miss Flynn: Right! Today we're going to line up before we come in the room. I want to see how quickly you can line up in silence. Five ... four ... three ... two ... one ...

The class are now lined up, but the students are still chatting among themselves. Miss Flynn coughs and looks at her watch, but doesn't say anything. She waits a moment to see whether they will become silent without any intervention, but they continue talking.

Miss Flynn: [*Apparently talking to herself.*] Oh dear. They're not silent. And that's what I want before I let them in the room, because I need to talk to them. Oh well, it looks like they're going to be spending some of their break time with me. What a shame. And they're such a nice class, although they are just too chatty. [*She sighs and looks at her watch.*] That's one minute wasted, so that's one minute at break time.

The class realize what is going on and the more observant students 'shush' the others. There is still some low-level chatter, though.

Miss Flynn: [*Looking at her watch again.*] Well, some of them are listening, but that's still two minutes wasted. Of course, I might allow them to win the time back if they can all be silent in five ... four ... three ... two ... one ... zero!

It works! Miss Flynn can now address the class and let them into the room.

Miss Flynn: That's excellent. Well done. Now, that is how we are going to start every lesson from this point onwards – lined up in silence, waiting outside the classroom. I've decided that you're becoming rather too talkative and I'm going to stamp it out. Right. I want you to come into the classroom quietly and sensibly. As soon as you are in your seats, I want you to get your books and pens out, and sit in silence, arms folded, so that I can take the register. The first person ready, sitting in silence, gets a merit!

The class hurry inside, and by the time Miss Flynn comes in, they are all waiting in silence.

Commentary on the good example

The teacher has decided to use a fairly light approach to deal with the problem, although with a touch of strictness as necessary. This kind of style is well suited to Year 7 students – if the teacher suddenly needs to clamp down on them, she could simply raise her voice slightly, or change her tone. When the students arrive, she is ready and waiting for them, her strategy already planned. The first thing she does is set the class a challenge, with a time limit, counting down from five to see whether this will work. It does to a certain extent, because the students are now in a straight line (useful because she can see all their faces). Unfortunately they are still chatting.

Now the teacher decides to use a rather unusual technique. She acts as though she is talking to herself, telling herself what she wants from the class, how they are failing to meet her expectations, how she does in fact really like them, and finally what the result of their continued chatter will be. By appearing to talk to herself, she is in fact thinking out loud, completely depersonalizing the sanction she gives. The students start to respond and, capitalizing on this, the teacher offers them a get-out clause of winning back the detention time. Finally, she again uses the countdown technique and this time it works.

Once the class is completely silent and attentive, the teacher can talk to them about why she wants them to line up in this way. She sets the standard for the future, so that they know what is expected of them when they come to her lesson next time. Lastly, she gives them a target to achieve, with a reward for the first to manage it (Year 7 generally love to compete) – to get into the room quickly and quietly and then sit in silence so that she can take the register. Notice how, throughout the encounter, the teacher remains relentlessly polite and calm.

A bad example

The class arrive for their lesson, chatting away happily. Miss Flynn is inside the classroom, doing some last-minute preparation. When she sees them starting to come in, she waves them back outside.

Miss Flynn: No, no, no! Get out! Out! I'm not letting you lot in here until you're quiet. Get back outside and wait for me.

James, a nice, quiet, well-behaved student is already sitting at his desk, getting his pencil case and books out.

Miss Flynn: James! Out I said! I can't believe it! What is wrong with you today? You're normally so nice. Pack your stuff up and get out!

James: But Miss ...

Miss Flynn: Don't you 'but Miss' me, young man. Just shut up and do what I say.

More students are arriving, and Miss Flynn backs them up to the door, waving her hands at them.

Miss Flynn: Outside. Outside, I said! I want you lot lined up and silent.

The class make a vague sort of line, but there is still quite a lot of talking.

Miss Flynn: Right, shut up you lot, I want to talk to you.

James is talking to the student behind him, telling her to be quiet for Miss Flynn.

Miss Flynn: James! Didn't you hear me? I said be quiet. That's the second time you've disobeyed me today. Right. You're in detention with me after the lesson.

James: But Miss ... that's not fair! I was only telling ...

Miss Flynn: Don't talk back to me. You were talking, now you're in detention. Now can you lot please shut up and let me get on with it.

By now the class are either engrossed in watching the confrontation between Miss Flynn and James, or are chatting among themselves because they are bored with waiting.

Miss Flynn: [*Starting to lose her temper.*] I said be quiet! SHUT UP!!!

The class quietens down, although a few of the more regular troublemakers are at the back, still talking.

Miss Flynn: Right, when you get inside sit down and be silent so I can take the register. OK? Come on then, in you come.

Commentary on the bad example

Right from the start of the lesson, it is clear that Miss Flynn is not well prepared for this encounter. If she does want to change her usual routine, this must be planned in advance, and she must be ready to interact with the class immediately they arrive. From the word go, when she flaps at them to leave her room, she is sowing the seeds for a negative lesson. In fact, her very first word is '*No*'! When they start to come into the room (as they are used to doing) she acts as though they are trespassing on her space. This inconsistency is bound to set up at least minor confrontations.

Her next mistake is to pick on poor James – a well-behaved student who is simply doing what he normally does, getting ready for the lesson! She immediately asks him what is 'wrong with him', a very negative comment, compounded with rudeness when she tells him to 'shut up'. Once the teacher has waved the students outside, there is already a feeling of disquiet about this lesson, and it is not surprising that they do not follow her instructions. Again, she is rude, telling them to shut up. She then picks on James unfairly – he is trying to get one of the other students to be quiet, but she accuses him of disobeying her and gives him an unearned sanction. If James was a confrontational type of student, this could have led to a more serious incident.

The class are now confused and bored – they had arrived at the lesson expecting consistency, and things are not turning out as normal. Because they are not fulfilling her (unrealistic) expectations, the teacher loses her temper. This does quieten the class down, but she then allows the students inside without having their full attention. At this stage, it seems to have been totally pointless for her to insist that they go outside and line up – she has achieved nothing! The 'troublemakers' at the back of the line have got away with their misbehaviour, and the lining-up activity is therefore pretty meaningless. At this point, it is likely that the class will take a long time to settle once inside the room, and they will have a negative view of the whole encounter.

Chewing gum

Age group: Year 9.
Details of the problem: Chewing gum is not allowed in the school. A few members of the class are consistently ignoring this rule. The same students are also proving to be among the more disruptive element of the group.

A good example

The class are working on an individual task. Mr Everall is going around the room, helping them. He notices that Sundip is chewing. He goes to

213

the front of the classroom, picks up the bin, and holds it under Sundip's mouth.

Mr Everall:	Sundip! Gum in the bin. Now. You know the rule.
Sundip:	But Sir! I'm not chewing.
Mr Everall:	Yes you are. Spit it out. NOW.
Sundip:	I've swallowed it, sir. Look. [*He opens his mouth wide.*]
Mr Everall:	I'll take your word on that, Sundip. But if I catch you chewing again this lesson, you're in big trouble.

Later on in the lesson, Mr Everall notices that Sundip is chewing again.

Mr Everall:	Sundip. I want you to come over here please. [*He walks over to the bin.*]
Sundip:	What, Sir?
Mr Everall:	Over here please.

Sundip comes over to where the teacher is standing.

Mr Everall:	See that?
Sundip:	What?
Mr Everall:	The bin.
Sundip:	What about it?

Mr Everall leans towards Sundip and speaks quietly in his ear so that none of the class can hear.

Mr Everall:	Put the gum in there NOW. And don't give me 'I'm not chewing', because I saw you. You can stay behind for five minutes after the lesson to clean up my room. Any more rubbish from you, and you'll be in a half-hour detention.

Sundip spits out the gum and sheepishly goes to sit back down.

Commentary on the good example

This Year 9 class requires a slightly different, harder approach than the Year 7s in the previous incident. Because there is a disruptive element in the group, it is essential that the teacher makes his control of the situation very clear. His first approach is to demand in front of the whole class that the student puts the gum in the bin: the class already knows the rule about no gum and this student is plainly disobeying. Although this might seem quite a minor problem, if the teacher clamps down on it now, his overall authority will be reinforced because he has shown himself willing to apply all the school rules.

As often happens, the student claims to have already swallowed the gum, thus making the teacher's demand void. Instead of getting into a big scene about this, the teacher warns the student what will happen if he is caught again. Later on in the lesson, the same situation arises. This time, the teacher takes a different approach, dealing with it in a more private way. He gets the student to come to him (always a useful way of showing your high status) and then demands that he put the gum into the bin, making it perfectly clear that this time, the student must not 'try it on'. He then sanctions the student as promised, making the punishment fit the crime, and warning him that any further disobedience will result in a longer penalty.

A bad example

The class are working on an individual task. Mr Everall is going around the room, helping them. He notices that Sundip is chewing.

Mr Everall:	Sundip? Are you chewing?
Sundip:	No Sir.
Mr Everall:	Yes you are. I saw you.
Sundip:	No I'm not, Sir. Look. [*He opens his mouth wide.*]
Mr Everall:	I saw you chewing. Don't give me that rubbish. Could you go and spit the gum in the bin please?
Sundip:	But, Sir. I'm not chewing.
Mr Everall:	You'd better not be.

Later on in the lesson, Mr Everall notices that Sundip is chewing again.

Mr Everall: Sundip. I thought you said you weren't chewing?
Sundip: I'm not. I'm just biting the inside of my mouth. I do
             that when I'm bored.
Mr Everall: Are you sure?
Sundip: Absolutely sure.
Mr Everall: OK then.

Commentary on the bad example

This example is 'bad', not because a confrontation occurs, but
because the student ends up getting one over on the teacher. In a
class where there are troublemakers, this can be a dangerous
precedent, because if a student gets away with minor misbehaviour like this, he or she starts to push the boundaries to see
exactly how far they can go before being sanctioned. It is your
decision as a teacher whether or not you apply rules such as the
banning of chewing gum. You need to ask yourself – is it worth
the confrontations that might occur? And can you use the rule to
demonstrate your control over the class in a calm and consistent
way?

The teacher's style here is very defensive. He asks the student
whether he is chewing, rather than stating that he has seen him
doing so. He also avoids sanctioning the student, perhaps because
he is nervous about what might happen if he does. In this
example, the student clearly wins the encounter – all the
'certain' statements are made by the student, rather than by the
teacher. The comment that Sundip makes about being 'bored'
hints at the contempt which this student feels towards the
teacher and the lesson.

The plasticine flicker

Age group: Year 2.
Details of the problem: Sally is a real handful. She is very lively, and
if she gets bored in lessons she starts to flick plasticine at the
other students. The teacher rarely sees her doing this, but the
other children in the class keep complaining, and at the end of

the school day, Miss Burn's carpet is always covered in little bits of plasticine!

A good example

The class are working in small groups on a weighing activity. They are weighing different substances to see which ones are heavy and which ones are light. Unfortunately, one of the things that they have to weigh is plasticine. Miss Burn is keeping a close eye on Sally's group. She notices that they are about to weigh the plasticine.

Miss Burn: Well done, red group. You've managed to weigh all these different things so far. What did you find out about them?

Ben: The tissue paper is really light, Miss.

Miss Burn: That's great, Ben. What else did you find out?

Robert: The metal block was very heavy.

Miss Burn: Excellent, Robert. What about the plasticine? Sally. Do you think that's going to be heavy or light?

Sally: Light, Miss.

Miss Burn: Are you sure, Sally? Shall we try it now?

Sally: OK. [*She weighs it.*] Oh. It's heavy, Miss.

Miss Burn: And when something is heavy, what could happen if we throw it at someone? Ben. What do you think?

Ben: You might hurt them, Miss?

Miss Burn: That's right. Now, Sally. Do you think it's a good idea to throw a metal block at someone?

Sally: Definitely not, Miss.

Miss Burn: And plasticine?

Sally: Well, you could just throw a little bit. Then it wouldn't hurt them.

Miss Burn: But what if it got in their eyes?

Robert: That would hurt loads! I got some soap in my eyes and it really hurt. Plasticine might be like that.

Miss Burn: And what would happen if we got plasticine on the carpet?

Robert: It could go all sticky. Look, Miss, there's some on the carpet here. Uggh!

Miss Burn:	Do you think it's ever right to throw things, Ben?
Ben:	Well ... you can throw a ball in the playground, Miss.
Miss Burn:	But what about in the classroom? What do you think, Sally?
Sally:	No. We shouldn't throw things at all, Miss.

Commentary on the good example

In this example, the teacher comes at the problem from a lateral direction. Rather than catching Sally in the act of throwing (which would have been problematic), she decides to approach the issue by discussing it, trying to make the children understand *why* they shouldn't throw things. She approaches the group just as they are about to tackle the plasticine, and immediately praises them for the way they are working, setting up a positive feeling about the whole encounter.

She discusses the activity with them, making sure they all contribute, and leading up to the issue of why it might be dangerous to throw plasticine. At no point does she actually accuse Sally of throwing plasticine, but what she does do is point out the problems that might be caused if anyone happened to do this. The whole issue is completely depersonalized, and Sally will hopefully be forced to reconsider her behaviour. If she does continue to flick plasticine, the teacher can simply refer back to this discussion, making clear the reasons for stopping the behaviour.

A bad example

The class are working in small groups on an art activity. They are making plasticine models of farm animals for a project. Miss Burn is helping green group when she gets hit on the head by a plasticine pellet.

Miss Burn:	Ow! Who threw that? That really hurt me. Sally? Was it you? I've seen you throwing plasticine before.
Sally:	No Miss. It wasn't me. It was Josh.
Josh:	No it wasn't. It was you, Sally, I saw you.

Miss Burn:	Sally. Not only do you throw plasticine at me, but you're also a liar. That's very naughty.
Sally:	I didn't throw it. Josh is lying.
Josh:	No I'm not. You're the liar. Liar! Liar!
Miss Burn:	Stop it! Both of you! Go and sit on the carpet. If you can't behave yourselves, then no fun activities for you.

Sally and Josh go to sit on the carpet. A few minutes later a fight starts between them.

Miss Burn: STOP THAT RIGHT NOW!

Commentary on the bad example

This encounter seems doomed to failure right from the start. Because the teacher has actually been hit by the pellet, she is emotional about the situation, rather than approaching it in a calm and rational way. Her immediate reaction is to accuse Sally. Although she may well be correct in doing this, it does seem unfair to blame her without any proof. Sally, probably embarrassed about her behaviour, tries to lay the blame on another student. Josh understandably feels aggrieved about this. He is then sanctioned despite having done nothing wrong. The incident ends with the children being punished, but the punishment deprives them of the chance to do their work. It would be far better to sanction them in a way that does not impact on their learning, but instead makes them address their behaviour.

It is hardly surprising that a fight starts between the two children when they are sitting on the carpet, bored, with nothing to occupy them. They are watching the others do a fun activity, and for Josh in particular this must seem very unfair – all he did was defend himself when he was falsely accused!

219

16
'Major'
Behaviour
Problems

The examples

In this chapter I look at some of the more serious behaviour problems that might occur in your classroom. These incidents can make the teacher feel extremely threatened and, after the event, can leave you in a vulnerable and unhappy state. Happily, in the majority of schools these events are relatively rare. By looking at ways of dealing with these serious incidents *before* they occur, I hope to arm you with the knowledge that you will need if you do face such an event in your own classroom.

When dealing with a serious confrontation, it's vital to ensure your own safety, and that of the students in your class. If a situation seems likely to blow up, never be afraid to use the 'ultimate sanction', for instance a red card that means the student must go immediately to a senior manager. Send a trusted student for help, too, if you feel it's necessary.

If you work in a school in which serious incidents are rare, then you might feel that the teachers in these examples are too lenient. It could be that, at your school, an instant punishment for a single swear word would be accepted with good grace. However, in some schools there are some very troubled children who need a more subtle approach, one that takes their backgrounds into account. In these situations, the instant and inflexible application of sanctions would lead to large numbers of confrontations and student exclusions. Again, the decision about when it is appropriate to be flexible must depend on the circumstances in which you teach.

Please note: because I want these examples to be as realistic as possible, I have included the swearing that often accompanies serious incidents. I have replaced the swear words with asterisks – I leave it up to your imagination to fill in the blanks.

The threat of physical aggression

Age group: Year 10.
Details of the problem: Colin is a very difficult student, whose temper flares easily and often. During a lesson, he becomes

involved in an argument with Patrick which quickly threatens to turn into a physical fight.

A good example

Colin and Patrick are arguing about who owns a CD. Colin claims that he lent it to Patrick, but Patrick disagrees.

Colin:	Give it back, you ******!
Patrick:	Get real, Colin. It's mine. You never lent it to me.
Miss Cook:	Colin. Patrick. I want you both to calm down please.
Colin:	He nicked my CD, Miss.
Patrick:	He called me a ******, Miss!
Miss Cook:	Look, I want you both to get on with your work. And I want you to stop using foul language before I have to punish you for it. Give me the CD, Patrick, and we'll sort this out at the end of the lesson.
Patrick:	No way. It's my CD.
Miss Cook:	Patrick. Give me the CD *NOW*. No arguing. And go and sit over there away from Colin please. [*She points to the far side of the classroom.*]

He hands it over grudgingly and moves to sit across the room. The boys settle to work, but a few minutes later they start arguing again across the classroom.

Colin:	I'm gonna get you after school, you ****.
Patrick:	Oh yeah? Well I'm gonna mash your head you stupid ******!
Miss Cook:	Right, that's enough. Colin, Patrick. Outside *NOW*.
Patrick:	I'm not going outside. I ain't done nothin'.
Miss Cook:	Both of you outside *NOW*. I mean it. Don't mess with me.

The boys and Miss Cook go outside the room. She stands between them so that they can't get to each other.

Miss Cook:	Right. We're going to sort this out now. I have the CD, and if there's any more rubbish about fighting from either of you, I'm going to give it to the head. Then he can decide whether or not you get it back. Patrick? What do you say? Are you going to get on with your work? No more nonsense?
Patrick:	All right, Miss.
Miss Cook:	Good. Very sensible. Right. You go inside I want to talk to Colin on his own. [*Patrick goes back in.*]
Colin:	I'm gonna punch him, Miss. I don't care what you say.
Miss Cook:	Colin. You are making me extremely unhappy with this attitude. If you punch Patrick, you'll get yourself into trouble. You'll probably be excluded again. Is that what you really want?
Colin:	No.
Miss Cook:	I want us to sort this out by talking about it. Tell me about the CD.
Colin:	My sister bought it for me. I lent it to Patrick, but he won't give it back. He's a ****.
Miss Cook:	Colin, I'm going to pretend I didn't hear that. But if you swear again, we'll go straight to the head of department and she can sort this out.
Colin:	Sorry Miss.
Miss Cook:	Right. Your sister's in Year 9, isn't she? Could we find her at break and check with her? If she agrees with what you say, then you can have the CD back.
Colin:	OK.
Miss Cook:	Right, Colin. Now I want you to sit out here to work for the rest of the lesson.
Colin:	Why? That's not fair.
Miss Cook:	Do you want to get into a fight with Patrick? No? Well, I'm saving you the temptation if you sit outside. We'll sort out your CD at break, OK?

Colin agrees. Miss Cook brings him out a desk and chair to work at, leaving her door open so she can keep an eye on him.

Commentary on the good example

The teacher intervenes quickly as the argument starts, hoping to stop it before it develops. Such early intervention can often prevent a minor confrontation spiralling out of control. She chooses not to punish the bad language that Colin has used, because she knows that this will only exacerbate the situation. These are Year 10 students, and for many of them swearing is the normal way of communicating anger – she feels that there is no point in making a big deal out of it. She needs to get the CD off the students quickly, because that will solve the problem temporarily – if she has the CD then she can decide what is done with it. If Patrick keeps the CD, it is likely that Colin will try to get it off him physically. Her tone is very clear and direct – she tells him to give it to her NOW, rather than asking him. She also separates the two boys, hoping that this will stop the argument immediately.

Unfortunately, the conflict resumes a few minutes later, and the teacher realizes that she must take further action to settle it. The boys swear at each other, and threaten physical violence. This is unacceptable, and the teacher removes them from the room to talk to them further. By doing this, she can deal with the problem away from the rest of the class. The class can get on with their work rather than watching her talk to the boys. Again, the teacher tells them very firmly that they *must* go outside – she will take no argument on this point.

Once outside, the teacher uses the CD as a bargaining tool while talking to the boys – if they do keep arguing she will pass it to the head. She hopes that this threat will calm them down. She deals with Patrick first – he is the less aggressive of the two and she has no real wish to punish him. After sending him back inside, she can deal with Colin in a more peaceful atmosphere. Unfortunately, Colin continues with his aggressive stance. The teacher is well aware of how easily Colin can be 'set off', and she maintains a very calm but firm manner with him. She points out to him what will happen if he does go ahead and hit Patrick. Then she allows Colin to tell his side of the story – by listening to him and taking his points seriously, she shows her human side and she also shows that she is willing to believe and trust him.

Colin swears again, and again the teacher chooses to ignore it, but this time she issues a final warning. She then offers a solution, one that is deferred to break time, when she will have a better chance to deal with the problem. She is aware that she needs to get back inside to her class now. Finally, she asks Colin to sit outside for the rest of the lesson, thus avoiding the possibility of further physical confrontation. Notice how firm the teacher's tone has been in dealing with this whole situation, while at the same time remaining calm and non-confrontational. She *tells* them what to do, rather than asking them, thus maintaining a feeling that she is in control, no matter how nervous she feels inside. Notice too how she uses their names repeatedly, ensuring that she has their full attention when she is talking to them.

A bad example

Colin and Patrick are arguing about who owns a CD. Colin claims that he lent it to Patrick, but Patrick disagrees.

Colin: Give it back, you ******!
Patrick: Get real, Colin. It's mine. You never lent it to me.
Miss Cook: Boys. Will you please stop arguing?
Colin: He nicked my CD, Miss.
Patrick: He called me a ******, Miss!
Miss Cook: [*Sounding very irritated.*] Look, will you both stop using such foul language and get on with your work now. Do you want to be in detention with me after the lesson? No? Well, would you shut up then and get back to work.

The boys grudgingly settle to work, but a few minutes later they start arguing again.

Colin: I'm gonna get you after school, you ****.
Patrick: Oh yeah? Well I'm gonna mash your head right now you stupid ******!

The boys are on their feet, taking up threatening postures.

Miss Cook: Right. Stop that now. Sit down.
Colin: You ain't gonna mash my head you thick *******!
Patrick: Oh yeah? Come on then, Colin. You think you're hard. [*He holds up his fists.*]
Miss Cook: WILL YOU STOP IT AND SIT DOWN!!

It is too late, the boys are already fighting, and the rest of the class is urging them on. Miss Cook tries to get to them to separate them.

The Class: Fight! Fight! Fight! Fight!
Miss Cook: WILL YOU ALL STOP IT AND SIT DOWN NOW!!

Commentary on the bad example

Notice how quickly the fight escalates here, because the teacher does not intervene firmly enough right at the beginning. Instead of *telling* the students what she wants, she *asks* them to stop arguing. She also calls them 'boys', instead of addressing them by name, which lessens the impact of what she says. She threatens a detention as a way of solving the problem, rather than moving into the quarrel and removing the cause of friction, the CD. She also asks them to 'shut up', rather than telling them to 'be quiet'. By reflecting their own attitude in this way, and using an irritated tone, she is more likely to add to the conflict than to dissipate it.

After a few minutes the conflict is still there, and the boys start arguing again. Because the teacher did not intervene sufficiently early, it is now too late for her to stop a physical quarrel taking place. Again, she tells them to sit down rather than moving in to separate them or to take them outside, away from the class. But it is all too late – the fight is inevitable.

Serious verbal abuse

Age group: Year 8.
Details of the problem: Nina has a major problem with managing her anger, and when she does get annoyed, she lashes out verbally, swearing at anybody and everybody, including the headteacher.

A good example

The teacher sees Nina passing a cigarette to a friend during the lesson. He is tempted to ignore it, rather than start a confrontation, but Annie has spotted it and pipes up …

Annie:	Sir! I just saw Nina give Charlene a fag!
Nina:	Shut ya face, ya boffin!
Charlene:	Or we'll get ya after school!
Mr O'Gara:	Nina. Charlene. I want you both to come here please. And bring your bags with you. [*He signals for them to come to his desk.*]
Nina:	I ain't moving nowhere.
Mr O'Gara:	I'll ask you again. Nina. Charlene. Come here now and bring your bags with you. That's your last warning.
Charlene:	Come on, Nina. I don't wanna be in detention with the old goat. [*They go over to his desk.*]
Mr O'Gara:	I'll pretend I didn't hear that. [*He stands up.*] Right. I'm going to give you one chance to hand me the cigarettes, nothing further said. Otherwise you're going to get in serious trouble, because I'll have to phone your parents and tell them about it.
Nina:	I ain't givin' you my ******* fags. And anyway, my parents know that I smoke. So there, you old ****.
Mr O'Gara:	Nina. Your language is appalling. And just because I'm an old goat, doesn't mean I won't be offended by it. [*The rest of the class laughs.*] Swear again and you're in detention. Now hand over the cigarettes. This is a one-time-only offer. Either hand them over or it has to go further.
Charlene:	Can we have them back?
Mr O'Gara:	Have what back? What are you admitting to having?
Charlene:	Oh. I see. Nothing. Here you go, sir. [*She hands him the cigarette that Nina has given her.*]
Mr O'Gara:	[*Crushing the cigarette and putting it in the bin.*] Thank you, Charlene, you may go and sit down. Nina? I want you to give me the rest of the packet.

Nina: No way, you ******* ******! They're mine!

Mr O'Gara: Right, Nina. You had your warning. That's a ten-minute detention with me after the lesson, and I'm going to have to report you for having cigarettes. I want us to go outside the room and discuss this further, before you get in more serious trouble.

Nina: I ain't comin' to your ******* detention. No ******* way. And I ain't goin' outside the room with you, you ****!

Mr O'Gara: OK, then. Your detention has now gone up to twenty minutes and I'm going to have to speak to your head of year about your appalling language. You know that swearing is not allowed, Nina, and you are continuing to break that rule. Let's go outside and discuss this further, shall we?

He walks over to the door, leaving Nina standing at his desk. Eventually, she follows him outside. He closes the door behind them.

Mr O'Gara: Right, Nina. At the moment you have earned twenty minutes in detention with me and a referral for being caught with cigarettes. You know that cigarettes are not allowed in school, and neither is swearing. I want you to give me the packet now, please.

Nina: No. [*But she is starting to calm down.*]

Mr O'Gara: Look, Nina. It's your choice. Either cooperate or you'll force me to send you to see the deputy head right now. Is that what you really want?

Nina: No.

Mr O'Gara: Then give me the cigarettes and let's go and get on with the lesson.

He holds out his hand. Eventually Nina hands over the packet.

Mr O'Gara: Right. Back inside. And don't let me catch you with fags again, eh, Nina?

Commentary on the good example

This is a tricky situation to handle: the students have cigarettes and this is clearly a serious breach of the rules. However, the teacher has to work with these students in the future, and he feels it is important to maintain a good relationship with them. Notice how he stays relaxed and maintains his sense of humour throughout the incident. As soon as the problem starts, the teacher intervenes by telling the two girls to come to his desk. Fortunately, Charlene realizes that the teacher is serious, and encourages Nina to do as he says.

The teacher offers the students a 'get-out clause' by saying that, if they give him the cigarettes, he will take the matter no further. Unfortunately, Nina immediately starts swearing at him. He deflects this by remaining calm and also gets a laugh from the class by referring to Charlene's insult. He warns Nina that if she swears again, she will be punished. He then deals with Charlene, the less confrontational student, who is willing to go along with his offer. Once Charlene has gone to sit back down, he can deal with Nina on an individual basis.

Regrettably, Nina swears again, and the teacher is forced to carry out the punishment that he has threatened. He also tells her that he will have to take the matter up with her head of year. He needs to get her away from the rest of the class so that her audience is removed. By walking over to the door, he leaves Nina stranded on her own, and she is forced to follow him rather than look stupid standing there at the front of the class. Once outside, the teacher manages to calm things down. He summarizes the situation, and explains what will happen if Nina continues to refuse to cooperate.

Notice that, throughout the incident, the teacher talks in a low-key, non-threatening way. When he is forced to sanction, he depersonalizes the punishment. He ensures that the decision to comply (or not) is put in Nina's hands, and this will hopefully limit the amount of damage done to their relationship.

A bad example

The teacher sees Nina passing a cigarette to a friend during the lesson.
He is tempted to ignore it, rather than start a confrontation, but Annie
has spotted it and pipes up ...

Annie:	Sir! I just saw Nina give Charlene a fag!
Nina:	Shut ya face, ya boffin!
Charlene:	Or we'll get ya after school!
Mr O'Gara:	Girls. Can you stop being so rude. And can you give me the cigarettes? You know they're not allowed in school. You're both in detention with me after class. I'm going to have to phone your parents after school.
Charlene:	That's not fair, sir! I didn't do anything!
Mr O'Gara:	Oh do be quiet, Charlene, and get on with your work.
Nina:	You can phone my parents. They already know I smoke. And anyway, I don't care, you ******* ******!
Mr O'Gara:	What did you call me?
Nina:	A ******* ******!
Mr O'Gara:	[*Shouting.*] Right, young lady! You're in trouble now! That's an hour's detention with me after class. Come over here and give me the cigarettes!
Nina:	Get stuffed you ****!
Mr O'Gara:	How dare you! [*He goes over to her.*] Give me those cigarettes now or else!
Nina:	**** off! I ain't giving you my fags you old ****!
Mr O'Gara:	[*Shouting in her face.*] Get out now! And don't come back!
Nina:	[*Getting up and shouting back in his face.*] I'm telling my mum on you! You can't talk to me like that you ******* *******! [*She storms out.*]

Commentary on the bad example

This confrontation ends very differently from the first example,
and it is unlikely that Nina and Mr O'Gara will be able to repair

their relationship. It is also probable that Nina will now be in serious trouble. The first mistake that the teacher makes is to talk to the students across the class, from his desk, rather than getting them to come to him. He immediately sanctions them both and tells them that he will call their parents. When Charlene complains, he dismisses her out of hand.

Nina swears at him, and he makes the classic mistake of asking her *'What did you call me?'* She, of course, is only too happy to repeat the insult! The teacher loses his cool and starts shouting at her, which is guaranteed to escalate the situation. Without warning, her detention is increased to an hour, and she is still expected to capitulate and give him the cigarettes.

Now the teacher moves into Nina's personal space, threatening her and shouting in her face. For a confrontational student, such an aggressive way of dealing with the issue in front of the whole class can mean only one thing – the student will explode right back at the teacher. Once again, she swears at him. When he sends her out, she leaves with a parting threat and a volley of abuse.

The dangerous object

Age group: Year 3.
Details of the problem: Rikky has been warned on previous occasions that he must not play around with scissors. The class have talked about why this behaviour is dangerous. However, Rikky still has a tendency to wave scissors around dangerously, and in the past he has cut the other children's hair and clothes with them.

A good example

Rikky has a pair of scissors and is threatening to cut Marilyn's hair with them. She has started crying.

Marilyn: Miss! Miss! Rikky's gonna cut my hair! Make him stop!

231

Rikky:	I'm only playing, Miss. I'm not really gonna cut her hair.
Miss Pirot:	Marilyn, could you go and set out the drinks for break time? That's excellent, thanks very much Marilyn. [*Marilyn goes to sort out the drinks.*] Now, Rikky. I want you to give me those scissors right this minute. Hand them over. [*She holds out her hand.*]
Rikky:	Oh, Miss! That's not fair. I wasn't doing nothing with them. I need them to cut my maps out.
Miss Pirot:	Rikky. Hand them to me right now please.
Rikky:	[*Starting to get aggravated.*] No. I won't. I can't do my work without them.
Miss Pirot:	[*Clapping her hands.*] Right! I'd like everybody to put down what they're doing and look at me. Looking at me and listening please!

The class put down their maps and their scissors and look at the teacher. She is now studiously ignoring Rikky.

Miss Pirot:	Right! I'm going to set you all a challenge to see how clever you are. What I'd like you to do is to tear around your maps by hand, and I want to see who can do it best. The winner gets a gold star and a sticker of their choice! I'm going to time you – you have ten minutes to finish this work. Ready, steady, go.

When she looks back at Rikky, he has started tearing around his map by hand. She quickly picks up his scissors without him noticing.

Commentary on the good example

Once again, the teacher's early intervention is crucial in preventing a more serious situation from developing. If she had left Rikky to his own devices, he might well have actually cut Marilyn. The teacher's first step is to remove Marilyn from the equation, by offering her an exciting alternative. This will also help distract Marilyn from being upset. Next, she demands that Rikky hand over the scissors. His response, that he needs them for his work, is in fact quite true. When she realizes this, and sees that he might become confrontational if she continues, the teacher quickly decides to take a different tack.

At this age, children are relatively easy to distract, and this is what the teacher chooses to do. She ignores Rikky, removing her attention from him, and getting the class's attention instead. She then offers them a challenge that means they won't have to use the scissors at all. She sweetens the contest with a reward that she knows Rikky likes – a gold star and a sticker. By the time she looks back at Rikky, he is engrossed in the challenge and she can subtly remove the dangerous object from his table. The teacher can talk further with Rikky about the safe use of scissors at another time.

A bad example

Rikky has a pair of scissors and is threatening to cut Marilyn's hair with them. She has started crying.

Marilyn: Miss! Miss! Rikky's gonna cut my hair! Make him stop!

Rikky: I'm only playing, Miss. I'm not really gonna cut her hair.

Miss Pirot: Rikky. I've asked you before and I'll ask you again. Can you please stop playing with the scissors? You know it's dangerous. Marilyn, do stop being silly and crying like that. He hasn't hurt you, has he?

Rikky: Oh, Miss! That's not fair. I wasn't doing nothing with them. I need them to cut my maps out.

Miss Pirot: Can you hand me the scissors now, Rikky, or I won't let you do the activity.

Rikky: [*Starting to get aggravated.*] No. That's not fair. I won't. I can't do my work without them.

Miss Pirot: [*Shouting.*] Rikky! Give me the scissors or there's no playtime for you today!

Now, both Rikky and Marilyn are crying. The rest of the class have stopped working to watch.

Miss Pirot: Now look what you've done, you silly children! Do shut up and get on with the work!

Rikky: I hate you!

Miss Pirot: And I hate you, Rikky! Leave the room now and go to stand outside the head's office. [*Exasperated.*] Oh, Marilyn, do stop crying!

Commentary on the bad example

This time, instead of removing Marilyn from the situation, the teacher accuses her of being silly: rather an unfair charge. When Rikky refuses to comply with her, the teacher quickly becomes annoyed and starts to shout, rather than remaining calm and dealing with the problem in a rational way. She threatens Rikky without warning that he will lose his playtime, rather than taking his complaint seriously, that he cannot do the work without the scissors.

When the rest of the class start to watch the incident, she calls both Rikky and Marilyn 'silly' and tells them to 'shut up'. This rudeness is bound to aggravate things, and Rikky responds by telling her he 'hates her'. She reacts rudely again, and the situation is only 'resolved' by sending him to the head's office, rather an overreaction to a problem that should have been dealt with easily. She is left with a class who are completely distracted from their work, and a student who is in floods of tears.

Part Six

WHEN THINGS GET
TOUGH ...

17

MANAGING
CONFRONTATIONS

Why do confrontations arise?

There are a whole range of complex reasons why confrontations arise. Sometimes the cause will be entirely outside of your control – a child will arrive at your classroom in such a tense and worked-up state that there is little you can do beyond containing the situation. Some children carry with them a huge weight of metaphorical baggage – horrible situations and events experienced outside of the school setting that make them far more likely to blow a fuse. Some students will have learned by example, from parents or guardians who react to problems in a confrontational manner. Wherever possible, within the bounds of confidentiality, it is worth your having at least some idea of the kind of home lives that your students lead. You can then be sensitive to their particular circumstances, applying the flexibility discussed at the start of this book.

At other times, though, the teacher will make a direct contribution to the confrontation. While it is not the teacher's *fault* that the child loses control, he or she does certain things that might exacerbate the situation. In your quest to manage behaviour better, it is important to understand how you might contribute to confrontations, so that you can avoid them whenever possible. Below are just some of the ways in which the teacher can create the climate for a confrontation.

- *The mood of the teacher:* When you begin a lesson in a bad mood, this attitude can filter through and put everyone in the room in a negative frame of mind. You might be unnecessarily picky or uncompromising with the students, and generate an atmosphere of tension and anger.
- *A sense of unfairness:* Children are very sensitive to actual or perceived unfairness. You probably feel (or hope) that you are completely fair all or most of the time. However, do be aware of how your own personal feelings about children can subconsciously come out in the way that you treat them.
- *Misunderstandings:* Sometimes we will accuse a child or a class of misbehaviour and be entirely in the wrong. For instance, I once caught some students passing around what I thought

was a note at the back of the room. When I insisted they hand it over, they refused and I got cross. In the end it turned out that they were all signing a 'thank you' card for me.

- *Playing to the 'audience':* When the teacher takes on a rude child in front of the whole class, this really does set the stage for a potential confrontation. While some students will back down, others will be unable or unwilling to do so, and will get themselves trapped into a slanging match with the teacher.
- *Lack of consistency:* Where a teacher is inconsistent, this can create a sense of injustice and consequently lead to tensions. It might be that the teacher applies the rules differently from other staff in the school. It could be that the teacher varies his or her expectations from day to day.
- *Prejudging the student or class:* Once a child gets a reputation, it can be hard to shift. Similarly, a class will sometimes be designated as 'difficult' by a number of staff. When the teacher meets a student or a class having preset expectations, it means the children are never given the chance to prove themselves. Again, this can create a sense of injustice and consequently lead to tension and confrontation.

How to avoid confrontation

Wherever possible, it is obviously far preferable to avoid getting into confrontations in the first place: they can only ever do damage to the relationship between you and your students. In addition, there is always the risk that a negative encounter might spiral out of control into physical aggression.

Problems can occur particularly when the teacher is tired and stressed. A student swears at you or behaves in a completely inappropriate way, and it is all too easy to confront the behaviour in a similarly hostile way, thus escalating the situation. Avoiding confrontation does not mean you avoid dealing with the issue, but rather that you approach the problem in a sensitive manner. When handling a confrontational student, try using the following techniques.

- *Be an assertive, confident and consistent teacher:* Where the teacher manages the class in an effective and assertive way all or most of the time, he or she will generally be rewarded with lower levels of tension.
- *Be aware of your emotional state:* On those days when you are tired or tense, have an awareness of how this might affect your classroom management skills. Minimize potential stress by keeping lesson activities simple and controlled. Make sure you take your breaks and leave school on time to get a good rest.
- *Keep difficult interactions private:* Learn to talk with and sanction students in a private way, so that there is no risk of them playing up to the audience.
- *Make an early intervention:* Keep an eye out for the early signs of any problems. If you notice an argument starting, or a student becoming restless, intercede straight away.
- *Know when to ignore low-level misbehaviour:* On the other hand, know when it is appropriate to simply ignore silliness, rather than making an issue out of attention-seeking behaviour.
- *Refuse to enter into tit-for-tat arguments:* Some students love to drag teachers into arguments – it means they don't have to work and they might even be able to deflect the blame for misbehaviour. Don't get pulled in – it is pointless and can lead to unnecessary tension. Remember – 'be reasonable but don't reason with them'.
- *Change the subject:* Try using a distraction to dissipate a potential confrontation. Just as, when a baby is crying, you might try pulling a silly face or shaking a favourite toy, so by changing the subject with your students, you could throw them 'off the track' of their aggression.
- *Defer the issue:* There will be occasions when you are involved in an interaction and it becomes clear that the student is simply not going to do as you ask, and instead is getting increasingly agitated or aggressive. In these cases, it can help to defer the whole discussion until a later time, for instance telling the child that 'we'll discuss this at the end of class'.
- *Be willing to apologize when you get it wrong:* If you do make a mistake, for instance if you're rude or unnecessarily aggressive

with a child, have the humility to apologize. This will earn you a great deal of respect.

How to deal with confrontation

Once a confrontation gets started, some students will find it incredibly difficult to back down. As the adult, and the professional person, it is the teacher's responsibility to try to deal with the situation in the best way possible. The ideal is for you to manage the situation so that the least damage is done to the relationship between you and your students, while at the same time ensuring the safety of every child in your class. The following suggestions will hopefully help you achieve this.

- *'Remove' the problem:* Often, confrontation is about a 'thing', whether this is a pencil case, a CD, a mobile phone, and so on. If possible, get the 'thing' out of the equation. Take care with using confiscation as your first approach – this can escalate tensions. Instead, insist that the child puts the item away in a bag before you are forced to take it away. Sometimes you might 'remove' the student, asking a child to step outside the room for a moment, to calm him or herself down. Make sure the student is supervised, for instance by a teaching assistant.
- *Take feelings and complaints seriously:* Sometimes it will be enough simply to listen to the child. Ask the student to describe the problem that has led to the blow-up and make the right sympathetic noises.
- *Know when to send for help:* There is no shame at all in sending a reliable child to get a senior manager if a fight breaks out in your room. Not only might this help you handle the situation, but it also provides you with a useful witness to what is happening.
- *Remain calm:* It's very difficult for a student to sustain feelings of anger if he or she has nothing to feed off. If you remain calm at all times, it will be that much harder for your students to maintain a confrontational manner. It will also demonstrate a powerful positive role model of how to handle aggression.

- *Pause for a moment:* When a situation erupts in your lesson, the temptation is to jump straight in to sort it out. Take a few seconds to think first – giving yourself time to calm down can help you handle a tricky situation in the best possible way.
- *Use a hypnotic tone of voice:* Your voice can be very helpful in calming tense situations. Use a slow monotone to dampen down heightened emotions.
- *Use low-key body language:* Similarly, non-confrontational postures and body language can help calm things down. Make sure you keep out of the child's personal space – not only to lessen the tension, but also to protect yourself from physical attack.
- *Make repeated use of names:* Repeating a child's name will help you get his or her attention and might even allow you to pull them back from the confrontation. Combine this with a low-key and hypnotic tone of voice.
- *Remember: it's not about win or lose:* Teachers can get trapped into feeling that they have to 'win' a confrontation. The reality is that nobody really wins, no matter what happens in the end. Your aim should be to calm things down, not to end up feeling that you won.
- *You don't have to make eye contact:* We are so used to having eye contact with our students and our classes that it can be tempting to get locked into a 'look at me when I'm talking to you' attitude. Sometimes, a better approach is to talk to the child without looking him or her directly in the eye. This applies particularly to children from some cultural backgrounds, who may perceive eye contact as rude and threatening.

Handling the aftermath

When a confrontation has taken place in one of your lessons, you may find yourself feeling shaky and upset. You might also suffer a dip in self-confidence and feel that you have somehow 'failed' as a teacher. A good school will understand that serious confrontations can have a severe impact on staff, and there will be support available to help you manage your emotions. The following suggestions should hopefully help you to cope and to bounce back quickly.

- Give yourself some time to recover – if possible, ask for your next lesson to be covered so that you get a chance to rest.
- Find support wherever it is available, whether this is from managers, a union, other teachers, or perhaps outside of the school environment.
- Try not to take the situation personally – a child who is verbally or physically abusive obviously has some serious problems.
- Try not to bear grudges – aim to give the child a 'fresh start' the next time you have to teach him or her.

18

Managing
Stress

I can't cope anymore!

Teaching can be an extremely difficult profession in which to work. It is emotionally, physically and psychologically taxing, and there may be times when you do feel as though you just can't cope anymore. No matter how hard you try, you may feel that you are making no headway in improving the behaviour of your students. This is extremely demoralizing. Day after day, you arrive at your job, only to face students who simply will not behave. You might begin to dread coming into work, knowing that you will have to face such a difficult day. At these times, it is important to differentiate between the inevitable ups and downs of a teaching career, and the signs of a more serious problem. Once you've identified exactly what the problem is, you can explore some suitable options for dealing with it.

What's the problem?

The feeling that you can't cope anymore can build up slowly, or it can arrive without warning one day, when you feel that you simply can't get out of bed and go into work. Sometimes, the problem is a temporary one, and one that can be dealt with relatively easily. On the other hand, it could be a more long-term issue, and one that will require more extreme measures to solve. Here are some thoughts about what the problem might be.

Seasonal effects

The time of the year can have a huge impact on your ability to cope with difficult behaviour. In September you will be fresh and full of energy, ready to deal with whatever the students can throw at you. Of course, this is the time when you most need this extra energy. It is extremely stressful to be meeting new people, learning new names, and, if you are new at your school, finding your way around the building, the systems, and so on.

Towards the end of the first term, energy levels fall low, the nights become darker and the students more fractious. Ask

243

yourself – is the feeling that I can't cope a symptom of general tiredness? Will things seem better at the beginning of a new term, when I've had a holiday and I feel refreshed and ready to face my students again? If this is the case, try to have a proper break from teaching during your holidays. Refuse to take any planning or marking home with you, book yourself a flight to somewhere sunny, and concentrate on recharging your batteries. That way you can plunge in with renewed vigour when you return to school next term.

Overwork

It could be that you are becoming excessively tired because you are overworked. If you take on too much outside of lesson time, this can lead to problems dealing with your classroom teaching. You may have family or other commitments that cause you additional stress and leave you too exhausted to deal properly with managing the behaviour of your students. Think very carefully about your extra-curricular responsibilities. Although these activities offer a welcome change from classroom teaching, and a good opportunity to get to know your students, they also mean that you have to stay late after a full working day. Your number one priority has to be your health and sanity – learn to say 'no' to demands on your time when your stress levels are too high.

The school

On the other hand, it could be the school itself that is the problem: your working environment can have a powerful impact on behaviour in your classroom. Are your school buildings rundown and uncared for? Is the whole-school ethos a negative and confrontational one? Is there poor continuity of staff and a management that does not support you properly? And is the whole-school behaviour policy ineffective in dealing with the issues that you face? If you have answered 'yes' to some or all of these questions, then it is likely that your school is struggling with difficult behaviour.

If this is your situation, make sure you turn to other staff for support. And if you feel that your personal situation is getting out of hand, and that you alone cannot even start to improve the situation at your school, then you will need to decide whether you are willing to stay. The most important thing is for you personally to stay healthy and happy – and you won't be an effective teacher if you are unhappy or ill.

Your personality

Different people react differently to different situations. Some teachers seem able to shrug off incidents of misbehaviour, putting any problems behind them and moving quickly onwards. Other teachers take the same kind of incidents to heart, and find it almost impossible to wipe them from memory. Many of us do get very emotionally involved with the job – it's almost inevitable when you are working with young people, some of whom lead very troubled lives. But if you are a sensitive person, you will need to learn to cope with your emotional responses, particularly if you teach in a challenging school.

What are the danger signs?

A certain amount and type of stress is healthy: it is essential in keeping us energetic and 'alive', and keeps us from becoming dissatisfied with our work. After all, you probably came into teaching because you would have been bored by a typical office job. Teaching offers many different challenges, and it can be the most wonderful career in the world. On the other hand, a difficult teaching job can be too much for some people to manage, and there is no shame at all attached to feeling that you cannot cope.

Stress is a response to a difficult situation, and when we are stressed we produce high levels of adrenaline. Originally, the production of adrenaline helped us in a 'fight or flight' situation, where our ancestors needed to be ready to flee from danger or to wrestle the proverbial mammoth to the ground. The problem in our modern world is that we become overstressed, producing all this adrenaline without any means of using it up.

As a teacher, you have to stay and deal with stressful circumstances, rather than running away or resorting to physical solutions. If your school situation is problematic, and your stress levels are too high, your health could be put at risk, and not even the most wonderful career in the world is worth that. The symptoms of stress vary according to the individual, but there are some common signs that you could look out for to check whether you are becoming excessively stressed by your work:

Physical symptoms
- *Difficulty sleeping:* If you are having difficulty sleeping, particularly on a Sunday night when you are preparing for the week ahead, you could well be experiencing high levels of work-related stress. Do you dream about your problem classes? And do your dreams become nightmares in which you can no longer cope?
- *Feeling sick:* That hollow feeling in the pit of the stomach is, I am sure, something that many teachers can relate to, and certainly all those who have worked in a school where there are serious behaviour issues. Do you feel sick when you are about to face your most difficult class, or classes? Or do you have that sick feeling all the time? If you do, it is likely that you are suffering from excessive stress.
- *Increased heart rate:* In addition to feeling sick, you might find that your heart begins to beat faster because of the production of adrenaline. Does this happen to you when you are about to teach? Again, a raised heart rate can be a symptom of stress.
- *Sweaty palms:* If your palms become sweaty in tense classroom situations, this could be a further sign that you are over-stressed.

Emotional symptoms
- *Loss of confidence:* When you feel that you can't cope with the behaviour of your students, it is easy to lose confidence in your teaching abilities. Your perception of what is actually happening in your classroom can become distorted, and the

problems you are experiencing might loom much larger than they are in reality.

- *Becoming defensive:* You might also find that you become overly defensive, expecting the worst from your students. This can be very counterproductive and can lead to a negative attitude towards your work and your children.
- *Bursting into tears:* All too often, I have seen teachers (including myself) reduced to tears in the staffroom, or even in the classroom. What other job forces this sort of humiliation on its workers? If you find yourself feeling overly vulnerable and emotional, this is probably a sign of very high stress levels.
- *Becoming snappy:* When you or your colleagues are stressed, the temptation to snap at each other becomes greater, particularly if you are all dealing with similarly difficult students. Again, poor relationships between the staff in a school can indicate a time of high stress, perhaps during an inspection or other stressful event.

How do you cope?

How, then, do you cope if your stress levels are high, and you feel that behaviour management problems are getting on top of you? Firstly, follow the advice given in this book. Many of the tips that I give are simple to put in place, but will make a huge difference to behaviour in your classes. The strategies could take a while to work, so don't lose heart if they don't make an immediate difference. With persistence, you will start to make inroads into your problems. In the meantime, here are a few specific ideas for managing high stress levels.

Use your support systems

In my experience, the staff who work in schools are wonderful at supporting their colleagues. Use all the support systems that are available to you: an induction tutor, a SENCo, a fellow teacher, a teaching assistant, plus friends and family too. Talk about your problems with someone sympathetic – sometimes all that is needed is a shoulder to cry on, or a caring ear in which to pour out your woes.

It can be very helpful to watch another teacher's classes, someone who you know has excellent classroom control. Although this option is usually only offered to newly qualified teachers, a supportive head might allow you to do some observations if you explain how helpful the opportunity would be. By watching how someone else copes with similar students to your own, you will pick up some useful tips that you can utilize in your own classroom.

If you watch a teacher who has been at the school for a while, don't forget the power of a good reputation. If you are new to the school, you will still be building up your own positive word of mouth. Similarly, if you watch a member of staff who has a management post (head of department, head of year, deputy head), remember that this responsibility will also have an impact on how the students behave.

Keep a perspective

In a difficult school it is sometimes hard to keep a perspective on what you are really achieving. At primary level, you will be wholly or mainly responsible for teaching one class – no one else is having to cope with exactly this mix of children. At secondary level, a major problem is that you never get to see the students in their other classes, and so you have no real idea of how they behave for their other teachers. Always remember, a badly behaved class is not necessarily a reflection of your talents as a teacher, but is a manifestation of many other contributing factors. Remember, too, that at the end of the day the world really is not going to end if your students won't behave themselves. Try to avoid blowing up incidents of poor behaviour into more than they really are. Bear this great quote in mind: 'Even in your worst lesson, nobody died.'

React from the head

Our instinctive reaction to rudeness or aggression is to take it to heart – we are human beings and not machines, after all. But every time teachers become emotional, this causes them stress and also shows the students that they can 'win' by misbehaving. Some students love 'winding up' their teachers, and when we react emotionally, they have succeeded. On the other hand, maintaining a rational, intellectual response will show the students that they cannot get at you. It will also help you think of ways to manage the situation in a calm and considered way.

Every time you feel your heart starting to race, and your emotions kicking in, take a moment to think about the situation from your head, rather than from your heart. Pause for a few seconds, to cut the link between your emotional response and your actual reaction. Respond in a logical, thinking way, rather than in a sensitive, feeling way. Here are a couple of examples to illustrate the point.

The disruptive student

Matthew is wandering around the room, disturbing the rest of the class and refusing to sit back down, despite being warned about possible sanctions.

Your heart says: *'Why won't he do what I say? The rest of the class must think I've got no control over him. I feel so helpless. Now I'm getting angry. WHY WON'T YOU DO WHAT I SAY, MATTHEW?!'*

Your head says: *'OK, this student is refusing to do what I say, but it's not my fault, it's his own choice. Now, what am I going to do about it? Well, first of all I'll stay calm, that's important. Then I'll warn him, and if that doesn't work, impose the sanctions that I've told the class about.'*

The uncontrollable class

Your class is an extremely difficult one, and they are totally refusing to settle down and get on with their work. They are making loads of noise and throwing paper aeroplanes around the room.

Your heart says: *'Help!!! They're completely out of control! What am I going to do!? Someone might hear them and think that I can't control my classes. I'm never ever going to be able to get them settled down and teach them! Why on earth did I decide to become a teacher?'*

Your head says: *'OK, things are going wrong here, but I'm not going to panic. First of all, it's not my fault, it's the students who have decided to misbehave. And everyone says what a difficult class this is. I'll try and apply the sanctions I've set, and if necessary I'll have to keep the whole class in. I know, I'll write ''whole class detention?'' on the board and see if that helps.'*

Take heart from small successes

When you are feeling really down, consider the small steps your children have taken that might make you feel proud. For a teacher in a difficult school, or working with a difficult class, getting your children to stay in their chairs may represent a huge achievement. Praise and reward *yourself* for these achievements, as well as your students. Teaching is a complex job, and there are many people who could not even start to make the progress you have made. Take a look at what your good students are achieving as well: often, when we are dealing with generally poor behaviour, it becomes easy to overlook the work and attitudes of our well-behaved children.

'The caring stops at five o'clock'

I was given this line by a teacher recently, and it does sum up perfectly the need to cut off from the job, especially if you are a sensitive soul. It is inevitable that, to an extent, you will take the job home with you. But if you wish to stay in the profession for the long term, you must accept that you cannot change the world. You will probably come across children whose lives outside of school are pretty miserable, but your main role is as a teacher and not as a social worker. Do the best that you can during working hours, but leave school behind when you head home for the day.

Don't be a perfectionist

You simply can't be a perfectionist if you're a teacher – the job is far too complex and multifaceted to get it right all the time.

When a lesson goes wrong, look for reasons by all means, but don't bog yourself down with excessive self analysis. If a student chooses to opt out of your subject, try your best, but don't beat yourself up about it. As long as you are doing the best that you can for your children, then you are doing your job. There is no point in dwelling on what is past and gone – keep learning, but always look to the future.

Take time out

There is no shame in sometimes making life easy for yourself, particularly if you are dealing with difficult children on a daily basis. On occasions, give yourself a break, perhaps by showing a video, or going to the computer room.

Take time off

If you are suffering from high stress levels, go to visit your doctor. It could be that you are ill, and that you need to take some time off to recover. You should not feel embarrassed or ashamed if you need to take sick leave. Teaching is an extremely taxing profession, and you will not be able to work at your best if you are tense and stressed. Above all, make your own health your first priority.

Get out!?

At some stage, you might have to ask yourself whether you are willing to cope anymore with your school, or with teaching as a profession. This is a personal choice that only you can make, but one that you will obviously want to consider long and hard. It could be that you have become disillusioned with your current school, but that changing to a job somewhere else will refresh your outlook on teaching as a career. Only you can decide.

Whether you do decide to change jobs, or to change careers, I wish you all the best in your future. And please don't forget, teachers make a huge difference to the lives of all their students. There are so many well-behaved children out there who need

251

your talents and your help. And your poorly behaved students are in desperate need of your care and attention to help them succeed, no matter how much they might push you away. So, follow the advice in this book, keep plugging away, and I promise you that you *will* be successful in 'getting the buggers to behave'!

Index